The Christian Faith:
A Catechism for the Curious

Eric M. Riesen

American Lutheran Publicity Bureau
Delhi, New York

The American Lutheran Publicity Bureau wishes to acknowledge with deep appreciation the work of Robert Benne for being the champion of this book, Frederick J. Schumacher for photographing the icon for the cover, Dorothy A. Zelenko for her ever-valuable assistance, and Martin A. Christiansen for cover design and internal page layout.

Paul Robert Sauer
Executive Director, ALPB

ISBN 1-892921-33-2

American Lutheran Publicity Bureau
PO Box 327
Delhi, NY 13753

Eric M. Riesen, *The Christian Faith: A Catechism for the Curious* (Delhi, NY: ALPB Books, 2015), 170 pp. rev.

Contents

On the Cover

The icon on the cover is of Christos Pantocrator (Ruler of All). It was written by Dmitri Andrejev, and is based on the original 6th century icon at St. Catherine's Monastery, Mount Sinai, Egypt. It is in the collection of Ronald Bagnall and was commissioned by the American Lutheran Publicity Bureau and presented to him upon his retirement as editor of *Lutheran Forum* in 2006.

The 9th century theologian, St. Simeon wrote about a similar icon: "At the moment when everybody's gaze is fixed on him, and when he too is gazing out at innumerable spectators, he maintains his eyes almost fixed in an unchangeable position, and each viewer has the impression of being personally regarded by him, able to enjoy his conversation and be embraced by him; no one can complain about being neglected" (*Etique* III).

Icons are not painted. They are (like books of theology) written. They are written in the hope of conveying divine Truth. This *Catechism for the Curious* was written with the hope that readers will be led to the Truth which is greater than we can conceive, yet which is truly and most fully revealed in Jesus of Nazareth whom Christians confess to be the risen Lord of all. Jesus is not primarily a teacher of truth. Rather he is the Truth. A book or icon is true only to the extent it reflects the truth and mystery of Jesus Christ. Apart from him "there is no God" (*Solid Declaration*, VIII, 81). The present work published by ALPB is a small offering written for those who seriously seek God's Truth. *Sola Dei Gloria.*

Acknowledgements

There are so many people to thank. First, I want to thank the congregation of Zion Lutheran Church, Pittsburgh (Brentwood). Over the last twenty plus years we've grown together. Thank you for your love, prayer, encouragement, and forgiveness over the years. Also, thank you for allowing and encouraging me to continue to study, to read, and pursue my theological interests. These chapters were originally presented as a Lenten series of sermons. Thanks to Keith Kirchartz and Cheryl Tracy who both proofread the final version, and to Bruce Randolph who read the manuscript in bits and pieces and offered insightful, humorous, encouraging, and humbling critique.

Great thanks to Dr. Robert Benne and the Rev. Dr. Gerald McDermott for taking time from their busy schedules to read the original manuscript and offering encouragement and suggestions. This book is a much better book because of them. Of course, all errors remain my own.

I owe a debt of thanks to the people at the American Lutheran Publicity Bureau who took a chance on a new author and agreed to publish this book. A special thanks to the Rev. Dr. Frederick J. Schumacher for providing access to his collection of icons as cover art.

Finally, thanks to our children, Erica, Paul (Brenda), and Tristan. The thoughts expressed in this book were often the things I was pondering when you asked me, "Dad, are you listening?" For those lapses in fatherly attention, I apologize. I trust that you know there were *never* any lapses in my fatherly love.

The greatest thanks to my wife Terry Lynne Newhouse Riesen, to whom this book is dedicated with love and gratitude. It would be incredibly difficult for a married pastor to do ministry without the support of a faithful spouse. I thank you most of all.

Eric M. Riesen †

June 11, 2015
The Feast of St. Barnabas, Apostle

*Grant, O God, that we may follow the example
of your faithful servant Barnabas, who, seeking not
his own renown but the well-being of your Church,
gave generously of his life for the relief of the poor
and the spread of the Gospel; through Jesus Christ
our Lord, who lives and reigns with you and the
Holy Spirit, one God, forever and ever. Amen.*

Preface

It is a pleasure to write the preface for Pastor Riesen's new adult catechism. I not only read the manuscript in preparation for publication, I actually enjoyed it. I enjoyed it for a number of reasons.

First, it is winsomely written. Pastor Riesen is a writer in a conversational style that is intimate without being chatty, clever without straining, and entertaining without being superficial. You will be delightfully engaged with his writing.

Second, Pastor Riesen draws upon many years of pastoral experience. The stories of his encounters with interesting people and events are always appropriate to the point he is making. His illustrations are from real life.

Third, he reads widely and uses that reading wisely. There are many complaints abroad that pastors no longer read scholarly material. The most you can expect them to do is read a journal article now and then. This is not the case with Eric Riesen. He has read widely and deeply. He is a scholarly pastor, and his catechism manifests that quality.

Fourth, he offers good orthodox Christian instruction of a Lutheran sort. When many pastors "go along to get along" with a changing cultural world, Pastor Riesen holds to orthodox Christian teaching and conveys it to the inquirer. This is solid Christian food for those curious about the Christian faith.

Finally, he writes from the "evangelical catholic" strand of Lutheran thought and practice. By that I mean that he sees Lutheranism as a reform movement within Western Christianity.

He embraces the "catholic" heritage of Lutheranism and teaches about it in this catechism. He appreciates the long sweep of Christian history, its liturgy, its sacramental life, its aesthetic sensibility, and its high view of biblical authority. His catechism teaches from the same tradition that the American Lutheran Publicity Bureau represents. The ALPB is proud to publish this book. It will be enormously useful to all pastors and congregations who want to teach inquirers the "straight stuff."

Robert Benne

Jordan-Trexler Professor of Religion
Emeritus, Roanoke College

Professor of Christian Ethics at the
Institute of Lutheran Theology

Board Member
American Lutheran Publicity Bureau

Introduction
A Catechism for the Curious
Spiritual, but not Religious?

*I believe in Christianity as I believe that the sun has risen
— not only because I see it, but because by it, I see
everything else.* — C.S. Lewis

*Both the credibility and the utility of the Christian faith
can legitimately be called into question if it fails to offer
a better account of reality than its rivals.* — Allister McGrath

Stephen Hawking, the great mathematician and physicist, lives in a broken body. Almost everyone has seen pictures of him slumped in his wheelchair. He can't move. His mind, however, is still sharp and active. He is an atheist.

On the other hand, there is Joni Erickson Tada. Joni is an author, speaker, and painter. She paints by holding a brush in her teeth. She also lives her life in a wheelchair because of a diving accident that severed her spine when she was sixteen years old. She is a Christian.

Religiously they're as different as night and day, but they both know what it's like to live in a broken body. Joni hopes to be healed in heaven. Stephen Hawking has no such hope. He probably would consider Joni's hope a pathetic delusion.

But there's something else that brings these two together. Each in their own way, despite their suffering, has kept a passion for life. It's this passion that inspires us. Stephen Hawking still writes bestselling books such as *A Brief History of Time*, and more recently, *The Grand Design*. Joni writes, speaks, paints, and encourages millions of people to trust in God's presence and love despite their sufferings. They've both lost a lot, but have maintained a sense of wonder and curiosity. Life is still interesting.

Stephen Hawking's passion stems from intellectual curiosity about the nature of the physical universe. Despite his lack of religious commitment, he is graced with intellectual gifts that sustain him. Joni's passion for life stems from her faith. She is graced with the hope of God. Her inspiration and creativity spring from faith. All of us recognize and admire the gifts of both these people.

Unfortunately, we live in a world in which, at least for many, life has lost its luster — quiet desperation on steroids. There are billions of people on this earth who are walking around in healthy bodies, but with a diminished passion for life. Famished people will feed on nearly anything — including each other.

The sociologist Max Weber saw this coming and famously dubbed it "the disenchantment of the world." People today are easily bored. This is why the entertainment industry continues to grow. It's an attempt to re-enchant our disenchanted lives. Movies, video games, computers, iPhones, iPods, the Internet, concerts, and restaurants catering to every taste, you name it, it's available. When life sucks, let's go shopping.

A few years ago some large Protestant congregations advocated "entertainment evangelism." The congregation became an audience, worship a concert. What mattered is that people *felt* entertained. If you wanted your church to grow, you'd better be entertaining. Let's go *church* shopping.

What the promoters of such things forgot was that the Christian faith, all by itself, is wonderfully life-giving and faith-inspiring. It's also fascinating, interesting, stimulating, mysterious, and *enchanting*. I am a Christian, but not because it provides endless hours of mindless entertainment as an escape from the "real" world. And, it isn't because I was steeped in the faith as a child or mindlessly accepted what the Bible or the Church taught. I wasn't, and I don't. I am a Christian because it has brought me a taste, or foretaste, of real life. What could be more entertaining?

Yes, like most people I struggle with periods of depression and doubt. The darkness is also real. Maybe it's God's grace or just plain stubbornness, but I haven't surrendered. I hate shopping.

This book is *not* about helping you to live your best life now, or seven secrets to successful living. This book is about wonder, and creativity, and compassion, and curiosity. It's about the reality of God who makes life infinitely interesting and worth living. A bored believer is an oxymoron.

The Imago Dei

The first book of the Bible tells us that humanity was created "in the image of God." We're at our best creating and at our worst destroying. What part of this do we doubt? The creative unbeliever is much better off than any type of destructive believer. People who destroy in the Name of God are deluded, deceived, and possibly even demonic. The devil destroys. Saints, true saints, create something beautiful in life.

Curiosity is part of creativity. It's terribly wrong when religions squelch curiosity and questioning. Are we that insecure? I've often had people admit to me that they were afraid to ask me, a member of the Christian clergy, a question for fear I'd get angry.

The ability to ask probing questions is what separates us from other animals. Cows are not curious about the big questions of life. Pigs do not pray. Beavers build, thoughtlessly. But the human capacity for curiosity and creativity is nearly infinite. Of course, our creative potential can, and often does, become twisted. Curiosity killed the cat. We could think about all of the possible ways creatively to kill a cat. The shudder you hopefully feel at that thought is a good thing.

All religions and philosophies (including science) are humanity's creative attempts to satisfy our curiosity about the fundamental questions of life. Philosophy uses reason to answer these questions and religion uses reason coupled with a spoonful (or shovelful if you prefer) of revelation.

Maybe you're thinking, "Well, I'm not religious, but I am spiritual." Okay, let's start there. If you're a spiritual person, then you're a curious person. You want to know more about spiritual things. The danger in being spiritual without being religious is that we may enjoy our questions so much that we never really think to find answers. We remain forever curious, but never committed. It's like a hungry person who enjoys looking for food, thinking about food, imagining food, but never actually finding and eating it. At some point the spiritual person must sit down to eat. True religion offers real food for spiritually hungry people. Junk religion is like junk food: immediately satisfying, but ultimately unhealthy.

If the answers to life's questions proposed by the Christian faith have truth in them, *then* we must make a commitment to be nourished by them.

A Catechism for the Curious

This is a catechism for the curious. A catechism is a series of religious questions and answers. Traditionally, in the Church catechisms are used to instruct people (usually young people) in the basics of the faith. So, for example, catechisms instruct a person on things like the Ten Commandments, the Apostles' Creed, the Sacraments, etc.

This catechism takes a different approach. Rather than beginning with sacred and *authoritative* religious texts (the answers), we'll begin with some of the basic questions of life.

First, we'll consider the question of God's existence. Then, we need to think honestly about the question of God's goodness. If God exists, but isn't friendly, then there's nothing to be gained from His existence. Christians believe not only that God exists and loves us, but also that God speaks to us. Primarily, God speaks through His Word. So, in chapter 3 we need to consider the inspiration and authority of the Bible.

Then, since most Christians understand that Jesus Christ is the central focus of the Bible, we'll think about the Incarnation of God and the doctrine of the Atonement (the cross of Christ). Christian faith teaches that on the cross God was redeeming the world from sin. We were "bought with a price" so that we would become new creatures.

What does new life look like? What is God calling us to do and become? What is our God-given purpose in life?

But it's not only life in "this" world about which we're concerned. The goal of this life is eternal life with God. What if resurrection is our destiny? Can we *really* believe in life after death? Isn't this just wishful thinking? And what about those whom we love who have died in friendship with God, where are they now? Can we have communion with the blessed dead? Should we want to?

Finally, after looking at these Big Questions and trying to discern if there's Truth in the answers proposed by the Christian faith, then we'll be better equipped to make an informed decision about our relationship with the Church.

If you're curious about Christianity, then no question, no matter how difficult or seemingly silly, is off the table. Allow your questions and curiosity to guide you. If the Christian faith is true (and I believe it is), then we have nothing to fear from the honest pursuit of truth.

I should also, perhaps with apologies to the reader, mention that this is a *narrative* catechism. This is, in many ways, my own story of coming to faith in Christ. It's the story I know best.

Bad Religion?

Apparently, human beings are religiously hardwired. It's something we can't help being — or doing. Every culture in human history has been religious. Of course, this says nothing about the truth or falsity of any particular religion. Crazy and corrupt religions are ubiquitous. Everywhere we look we can find kooky Christians, jaded Jews, mad Muslims, hateful Hindus, and bad Buddhists. And bad religions of every stripe always give bad answers to good questions.

Many suggest that the best thing to do is to get rid of religion altogether. As the famous 18th century French writer Denis Diderot famously said, "Men will never be free until the last king is strangled with the entrails of the last priest." He was not the first, nor the last person, to share this anti-religious sentiment. Karl Marx sought to abolish religion and construct an atheistic society. It didn't work. Marx's anti-religion became a religion complete with a set of dogmas and at least one incorruptible sainted communist corpse — Lenin's. Human beings, for better or worse, are incorrigibly religious.

Christianity is, as traditionally understood, a religion. Like all religions it has a particular set of values and beliefs which propose answers to life's deepest questions. But so do the Moonies (the Unification Church). The real question is, "Are these answers true?" Even more importantly, "Does Christianity provide the best, most authentic, answers?"

What about other "respectable" religions and philosophies? It's a big world filled with all kinds of answers to life's questions. Isn't it the height of arrogance to suggest that Christianity alone offers the *truest* answers? It smacks of intolerance to suggest that Christianity is truer than, let's say, Buddhism. In our post-modern world this may look impossibly, hopelessly outdated or simply out-of-touch.

My suggestion? Let's evaluate the claims of any religious tradition by looking at its best, most noble representatives. We could, for example, study the history of Christian kooks, heretics and hypocrites; but that would be like studying literary history by looking at the worst books ever written. Or we could study the history of film *only* looking at the worst movies ever made.

I once attended a showing of some of the cinematic sins of Hollywood. It included such blockbuster hits as *Robot Monster* and *Attack of the Killer Tomatoes*. It was *terrible*, and it would be ridiculous to judge all movies by these examples. Similarly, it is a great mistake to evaluate religion in this way. Consider the religion of Islam. Many today are tempted to evaluate this religion by *only* looking at the atrocities of the Islamic State. This evaluation is skewed and distorted.

In this study, our guides into the Christian faith will be some of its best, wisest, and most articulate representatives. Saints offer a much better window into the soul of a religion than hypocrites.

The Church Divided

Of course, not even saints always get along. Saints are also sinners. The Church is a body divided. Often, these divisions are based more upon misunderstanding and bigotry rather than truth. I sometimes hear people say things like, "Catholics worship statues," or "Protestants don't believe in good works." These are caricatures. Yes, there are serious differences which separate us. But there are also misunderstandings and malice involved. There is no excuse for bearing false witness. The lack of love evident among some Christians is scandalous.

I write as a Lutheran Christian. This theological tradition forms my faith in significant ways. The reader will note my Lutheran leanings throughout. However, my faith would be impoverished if I failed to recognize the gifts which other Christian traditions bring to the table. Below is a diagram that gives a broad and general outline of Christianity's 2000-year history and shows the major divisions within the Christian Church.

A Snapshot of the Divided Church

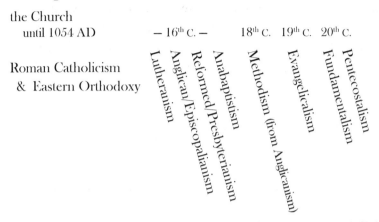

the Church
until 1054 AD   — 16ᵗʰ C. —   18ᵗʰ C.   19ᵗʰ C.   20ᵗʰ C.

Roman Catholicism
& Eastern Orthodoxy

Lutheranism
Anglican/Episcopalianism
Reformed/Presbyterianism
Anabaptistism
Methodism (from Anglicanism)
Evangelicalism
Fundamentalism
Pentecostalism

It is important to understand that for all the diversity and division which exist, there is a common faith that unites these traditions. It's what C.S. Lewis called *Mere Christianity*. This is an introduction to the faith that unites Christians. We'll explore the Christian faith in its *catholic* fullness. The word catholic (note the lower case "c") means the beliefs shared as the "cumulative consent" of *all* Christians across time. It is the faith confessed by Christians in different traditions and denominations when they recite the Apostles' or Nicene Creeds. The importance of confessing this "catholic" faith with the words of these *specific* creeds is significant:

> It is very important that these creeds and no other be recited ... in public worship. The substance of our ecumenical creeds goes back to apostolic times, and their precise formulations go back to the patristic era. They are affirmations of a faith that have been tested and achieved consensus in the ecumenical church.... The creeds are called "symbols" because they provide the identity of faith, just as a flag identifies a country.... The individual believer is able to find his or her ecumenical identity and solidarity with the church catholic when one of the ancient ecumenical creeds is recited in the liturgy.[1]

---

1. Frank C. Senn, *Lutheran Identity: A Classical Understanding* (Minneapolis: Augsburg/Fortress, 2008) 46.

Why are these creeds, and only these creeds, so important? Some people think that we need to bring the Christian faith into the 21st century and update the creeds. They are old, very old. They're ancient. In our society we spend billions of dollars each year to look young. Shouldn't the Church do the same? After all, these creeds were written by unenlightened people. Heaven was up and hell was down. So Jesus ascended and descended on a spiritual elevator in a three-story universe. It's like the Church saying, "Please check your brain at the door."

But here's a secret. The people who hammered out these creeds didn't believe that Jesus literally ascended and descended like a hot air balloon. They knew they were using metaphorical language to teach theological and spiritual truths. It is true that Jesus "ascended to the right hand of the Father," but no serious ancient theologian believed that God literally had a right hand. So when the Church asks us to confess these specific creeds, it's asking us to use our brains. Yes, we are asked to think.

Second, if we're really blessed (lucky if you're not particularly religious) we'll get 70 or 80 trips around the sun on this big blue ball. Much of that time will be spent eating, sleeping, waiting in traffic, and watching television. So we only have a limited amount of time to figure things out. This is true whether or not we're talking religion, politics, mathematics, or jigsaw puzzles.

In any field of study, why would I start from scratch? If I study biology, Darwin may have something valuable to teach me. Or, if I want to study physics, Newton and Einstein are helpful. The study of Christianity is no different. G.K. Chesterton said that a tradition is a "democracy in which the dead have votes." He's dead, but he was also right. The dead have voice and vote in the Christian faith. Any thinking person would admit that the dead have voice and vote in every other field of human knowledge. Some of my favorite teachers have been dead for centuries.

Third, I'm convinced that if you locked up a group of Christians, gave them Bibles, fed them only soda crackers and water until they wrote a brief summary of the most important beliefs of Christian faith, they would write something like the Apostles' or Nicene Creeds.

Finally, Christians believe that God did not abandon them to their own wits and devices after Jesus ascended to the right hand of the Father. He promised that he would send the Holy Spirit (Acts 1). According to the gospel of John, Jesus explicitly said, "I have many other things to say to you, but you cannot bear them now. When the Spirit of truth comes, he will guide you into all truth" (John 16:12-13). And remember, it's not the individual, solitary Christian all alone by herself who is given this promise, nor the individual congregation or denomination. The "you" to whom the promise is given is plural. It is the Church catholic which is promised God's guidance. It is the Church which seeks to proclaim, teach, and confess the "living faith of the dead."

Therefore, the catholic Church is bigger than any one expression of it. The Church exists (and often thrives) outside of any one Christian denomination. In the past, when the culture was friendlier to Christian beliefs and values, it was easier to live in our separate denominational families. We could build theological walls protecting the pure faith which we supposedly possessed in isolation from other Christians.

Things have radically changed. We live in a post-Christian world. It is folly not to recognize this. Christians who share the catholic faith must work towards greater unity so that we can better bear witness *together*. I do *not* mean to suggest that we sweep all theological disagreements under the rug and just "love each other." I do mean to suggest that those who truly confess the catholic faith in its fullness share a great deal in common. Our disagreements pale in light of catholic Truth.

The 5th century theologian, Vincent of Lerins, said that all Christian doctrine should be evaluated and judged in light of

18

what had been believed "everywhere, always, and by all."[2] So, when I preach a sermon, it should echo and reflect the faith of a Great Tradition of faith, and not simply my own personal ideas, experiences, and opinions.

Certainly my sermon reflects my own theological understandings as a Lutheran and my personal life experiences. But, it's not *my* own personal faith which I preach. It is the faith of the Church catholic which I personally confess which must be preached.

This does not mean that Christians simply mimic or parrot what others have said. Again, creativity is a good, God-given, gift. There are always new ways to understand and speak Christian truth. But, the voice of contemporary Christians must echo the Voice of God heard by the Old Testament Prophets, the New Testament Apostles, the Church Fathers, all the saints and teachers of the Church. Any true reform (change) must echo the consistent voice of our spiritual ancestors. Joseph Cardinal Ratzinger, who is now Pope Emeritus Benedict XVI, makes a point that all Christians need to hear:

> The reform that is needed at all times does not consist in constantly remodeling "our" Church according to our tastes, or in inventing her ourselves, but in ceaselessly clearing away our subsidiary constructions to let in the pure light that comes from above and that is also the dawning of pure freedom.[3]

---

2. Vincent of Lerins, *Commonitory*, XXII.27.

3. As quoted by Avery Cardinal Dulles, "True and False Reform," *First Things* 135 (August/September, 2003): 17.

Questions for Discussion

1. If you're reading this with a group, take some time to share names, and stories of faith. What was your religious upbringing? What are your earliest memories of the church? Are they positive or negative?

2. What are you most curious about concerning the Christian faith?

3. If you weren't raised in the Church, what memories do you have about religion? Were they positive or negative?

4. What brought you to this particular congregation? What questions do you have about this particular denomination?

5. What would you change about the Church? What do you like least? Most?

6. Do you have any particular questions about Church History? Or the history of a particular denomination?

Chapter 1
Does God Exist?

There is in a very real sense the presence of the absence of God. — G. K. Chesterton

My discovery of the Divine has been a pilgrimage of reason and not of faith. — Anthony Flew

I was out making a few pastoral calls and stopped to see a family who had a very sick child. The child was born with a rare, life-threatening, genetic disease. On that day the family wasn't home, but as I turned to leave, a car raced into the driveway. It was the grandfather. He'd been watching his sick grandson. The child had a seizure in the car. The grandfather stopped the car, and pulled the limp body of this little boy from the car. He held the child to his chest crying out, "Something's wrong!" I stood there not knowing what to say. Finally I sputtered out, "Is there anything I can do?" Thinking, should I call the EMS? Fall on my knees and pray for a miracle?

I'll never forget the look on that man's face. He was desperate, angry, confused. "Yes, you can make this go away! You can tell God to take it away! Why doesn't he take it away?" Then he quickly and more quietly added, "I believe in God, but sometimes I wonder."[4]

---

4. Recently I met this man again. I'd last seen him at his grandson's funeral. What surprised me, as it often does in terrible situations like this, is that this family did not turn away from God in anger. Actually, he told me that their faith had grown through this ordeal. It's also incredibly significant to know that another grandson, the brother of the little boy who died, was diagnosed with the same disease.

Stories like this could be repeated millions of times. I have stood by the sickbeds and graves of many people. People for whom we prayed, asking God to heal them, but they were not healed. When we're honest, we all sometimes begin to ask: Does God care? Is God really there? Why doesn't God do something? Does God exist?

The God in Whom I Do Not Believe

When someone tells me that they do not believe in God, I often ask them to tell me about this God in whom they do not trust. Often they do this with a certain amount of anger. While I understand this anger, if God doesn't exist, who are we angry at? The God who is the target of their anger tends to be rather small and spiteful. I don't believe in that god either. Who is the God in whom Christians believe?

To answer this question it's important to recognize that when anyone writes or speaks about God (including me!) anything that person says about God is inadequate. The God of *classical theism* is always more than we can think or imagine. God is *not* simply the greatest being we can imagine among lesser beings we know. God is the source and summit of Being itself.

Gregory the Great (ca.335-395 A.D.) once wrote that, "any man who entrusts to language the task of presenting the ineffable Light [of God] is a liar; not because of any hatred on his part of the truth, but because of the feebleness of his instrument for expressing the thing thought of." So, at the risk of unintentionally speaking falsehoods, in this chapter I want to try to say something true about God while keeping in mind that language can never capture God. God is always greater than, and other than, we think or imagine. Any divine Being we could imagine, one that could fit nicely between our two ears, would *not* be God. It would be an idol of our own imagination.

The medieval theologian Meister Eckhart (c.1260-1328) tried to highlight the mystery of God by insisting that God alone exists. Everything else "borrows" its existence from

God.[5] God does not so much exist as God is Existence itself. Nothing would exist apart from God if God did not will it to exist. God, so to speak, "makes room" (the Universe) for things to exist in and through Him, but still separate from Him. David Bentley Hart gets to the heart of the problem:

> [T]he most pervasive error one encounters in contemporary arguments about belief in God ... is the habit of conceiving God simply as some very large object or agency within the universe, or perhaps alongside the universe, a being among other beings, who differs from all other being in magnitude, power, and duration....[6]

Again, God is not the just the Biggest Being. God is altogether "Other" Being. If we envision God as the "Big Guy in the Sky," then our vision needs radical correction.

Second, if this is true, then how can we say or know anything about God? The best advice would be to remain silent. It's all a Big Mystery. As mysterious as God truly is, the Christian faith teaches that the wholly Other entered into our history through the life, death, and Resurrection of Jesus Christ. Jesus is the wholly Other become wholly human. He is, both God and human, God's clearest Self-revelation. If this is true, then something true can be known about the mystery of God.

Coming to Believe in the Existence of God

I did not always believe in God. Later, I'll tell a little about how I became a Christian and note that it was as if God "sneaked" up on me through the Word. Reading Scripture, talking to Christians, and beginning to attend worship were all ways by which God hooked me. When I reflect upon my journey, it is more like God found me than that I found God. It turned out that I was like a treasure hidden in the field for

---

5. David B. Burrell, "Analogy, Creation, and Theological Language," *The Theology of Thomas Aquinas* (Notre Dame, IN: University of Notre Dame Press, 2005), 87.

6. David Bentley Hart, *The Experience of God: Being, Consciousness, Bliss* (New Haven and London: Yale University Press, 2013), 32.

which God had sold everything to purchase. You, who happen to be reading this, are also that treasure.[7]

My efforts to find God were in reality just a sign of God's efforts to find me. The honest doubts and sincere questions I had were the stirrings of faith. In other words, paradoxically it is God's grace that causes us to search for Him *in order that* He might find us!

In this chapter we'll delve into the honest doubts and sincere questions about the existence of God. In doing so it's important that we take a hard look into the dark side of reality: the places where God seems most absent and most silent.

It is often noted that the Bible, the book inspired by God, never tries to prove that God exists. For the writers of the Bible, God's existence was rather obvious. Only the fool could say that there was no God.[8] But in our modern world, God's existence is, at least for many people, not so obvious. And it is not only fools who question God's existence, but very intelligent, kind, and moral people too. Recently, many books have been published that seek to discredit and deny belief in God's existence.[9] Why do these authors disbelieve in God? What difference does it make?

If God Does Not Exist

To walk away from faith in God is to chart a particular course in life. It is a decision that should not be made lightly or in

---

7. Cf. Matthew 13:44 in which Jesus compares the kingdom of heaven to a person who finds a treasure buried in a field and then sells all he has to purchase the field (and the treasure). While the parable applies to anyone who finds the treasure of God's kingdom, it must also certainly apply to Jesus who "sold" everything to gain our salvation.

8. Psalm 53:1.

9. A partial list includes the following: Richard Dawkins, *The God Delusion* (Boston, Houghton Mifflin, 2006); Daniel G. Dennett, *Breaking the Spell* (New York, Penguin Books, 2006); Michel Orfray, *Atheist Manifesto* (New York, Arcade, 2007); Victor J. Stenger, *God: The Failed Hypothesis* (Amherst, New York, Prometheus Books, 2007).

haste. While all of us have questions and doubts, the outright rejection of God (at least in my opinion) raises more questions than it solves. Consider this parable of modern unbelief:

> It is a peculiarly twentieth-century story, and it is almost too awful to tell: about a boy of twelve or thirteen who, in a fit of crazy anger and depression, got hold of a gun somewhere and fired it at his father, who died not right away but soon afterward. When the authorities asked the boy why he had done it, he said that it was because he could not stand his father, because his father demanded too much of him, because he was always after him, because he hated his father. And then later on, after he had been placed in a house of detention somewhere, a guard was walking down the corridor late one night when he heard sounds from the boy's room, and he stopped to listen. The words that he heard the boy sobbing out in the dark were, "I want my father, I want my father."[10]

Modern people are sometimes like that boy. In killing the Father (atheism) we have lost the relationship that tethers us to meaning, purpose, and morality. Untethered from these things, there is every cause to weep. If there is no God, then the universe is *graceless*, merciless, unforgiving, and even irrational.

Once, when I was taking a class at a Roman Catholic seminary, someone asked the professor, a Benedictine Monk, about the existence of God. I will never forget that Monk's response. He paused for a moment, looked at the student who had asked the question, and said: "If there is no God, then I'm taking the bridge."

Atheism is not just the rejection of a religious dogma, "It is the reversal of a subconscious assumption in the soul; the sense that there is a meaning and direction in the world it sees."[11] A

---

10. Frederick Buechner, *The Magnificent Defeat* (New York, Seabury, 1979), 65.

11. G.K. Chesterton, *The Everlasting Man* (Dodd and Mead, 1925; San Francisco, Ignatius Press, reprinted 1993), 162.

world devoid of meaning and direction is a world in which no *rational* person would desire to live.

Some will take exception to this. There are certainly happy and well-adjusted atheists who do not plan on taking the proverbial bridge. They could point a finger to the insanity sometimes inspired by faith in God. They might argue that if we could rid ourselves of religious irrationalities and become more reasonable, then we could begin to work together to solve the problems of the world and make it more livable. To quote the self-professed atheist Sam Harris, "I know of no society in human history that ever suffered because its people became too reasonable."[12]

But is this true? Is human reason, shorn of the absurdities of religious faith, the best hope for our world? Is faith a delusion? Less a reality than an escape from reality? Or even "the devil's masterpiece"?[13]

A Little Critique of Pure Reason

To answer these questions we need to think more deeply about the limits of what we can truly know by "pure" reason alone. The obvious problem is that human reason is never pure. We are all motivated by emotions, ambitions, prejudices, presuppositions, and a general self-centeredness which Christians call sin. This is true for both believers and unbelievers.

From the Christian perspective the reality of sin makes "pure" reason a rather quaint, unrealistic, and simplistic assumption. "It is important," wrote the late Richard John Neuhaus, "to expose the fallacious value-neutrality of those who claim to argue from a tradition-free and autonomous rationality."[14] Reason is never autonomous. Thinkers like Sam

---

12. Ibid., Harris, 231.

13. Ibid., 226.

14. Richard John Neuhaus, *American Babylon: Notes of a Christian in Exile* (New York, Basic Books, 2009), 101.

Harris would have us believe that they are *only* motivated by reason, which is nothing less than "the guardian of love."[15] However, while the human capacity to use reason has led to many blessings, very reasonable people have done some very unloving things.[16] As Pope Emeritus Benedict wisely writes, "deleting faith in God, however one may try to spin or turn it, ultimately deprives moral values of their grounding."[17] Where there is no moral grounding, you can be sure that the killing fields are not far away.

The "new atheists" may not like this reasoning, but you can't have your cake and eat it too. If scientific reason is the *only* criterion by which we should make moral judgments, then reason must simply be silent before the atrocities committed by hyper-rational people. It does no good to tout the glories of human reason and then complain when reasonable people commit heinous crimes *reasonably*. After all, in a totally rationalistic world, a world of "pure" reason, words like "heinous" have no objective meaning. Moral judgments are value statements. In pure scientific naturalism, ethical statements about good and bad or right and wrong "have no moral meaning."[18]

Christianity has always sought to bridge the gap between faith and reason. The Christian faith celebrates God's gift of reason, but with this difference noted by David Bentley Hart:

> Reason, in the classical and Christian sense, is a whole
> way of life, not the simple and narrow mastery of certain

---

15. Ibid. Harris, 190.

16. When we think of people who sought to build an ideal society based on human reason alone without God, the first names that spring to mind are Stalin, Mao, or Pol Pot. These men attempted to form ideal societies that were reasonable according to the strict and brutally logical dictates of atheistic Marxism. They used "pure" reason ruthlessly.

17. *The Essential Pope Benedict XVI: His Central Writings and Speeches*, ed. by John F. Thornton and Susan B. Varenne (San Francisco, Harper, 2007), 11.

18. Hans O. Tiefel, "Individualism vs. Faith: Genetic Ethics in Contrasting Perspectives," in *Genetic Testing and Screening* (Minneapolis, Kirk House, 1998), 135.

techniques of material manipulation, and certainly not the childish certitude that such mastery proves that only material realities exist. A rational life is one that integrates knowledge into a larger choreography of virtue, imagination, patience, prudence, humility and restraint.... [C]harity is required for any mind to be fully rational.[19]

Reason governed by faith and love is a beautiful thing, but reason devoid of these virtues is dangerous. The wisdom of G.K. Chesterton is apropos: "The madman is not the man who has lost his reason. The madman is the man who has lost everything except his reason."[20]

To limit what we believe "only" to what rationalistic and materialistic science can "prove" (known in philosophy as logical positivism) leaves us spiritually, intellectually, ethically, and existentially bankrupt. To know reality only through what can be discerned through the lens of empirical science is to limit ourselves to light from only one color of the spectrum — albeit, a *very* important color of the spectrum. This is kind of like a fisherman who uses a net with a four-inch mesh. He never catches anything other than fish which are larger than four inches. He might therefore surmise that fish smaller than four inches do not exist. So human scientific reasoning can capture many, essential truths, but to assume that it captures *every* truth is nonsense.

Consider the simple act of a kiss. Science, the realm of rational inquiry, could conduct a strictly monitored scientific study to explain what is rationally involved when two people kiss. We could seek to understand the hygiene (or lack thereof) in a kiss. After all, "swapping spit" (to borrow a phrase made popularized by the movie *On Golden Pond*) is not without health risks.

---

19. David Bentley Hart, *Atheist Delusions: The Christian Revolution and its Fashionable Enemies* (New Haven and London: Yale University Press, 2009), 236.

20. G.K. Chesterton, *Orthodoxy* (New York: Doubleday, The Image Books Edition, 2001), 13.

We could also conduct a cross-cultural study of intimacy to determine the cultural and religious factors that determine the how and when of a kiss. It might also be of interest to determine the evolution of a kiss. It could be argued that the kiss has evolved due to biological pressures to reproduce the species. A kiss was a way to determine the readiness of the female to receive the male. The tongue being used in a phallic manner by which the female would indicate her receptivity to the male. Thus the evolution of "deep" kissing.[21] There are many ways we could scientifically study the kiss, but still never understand it. As C.S. Lewis warned us, we are increasingly becoming "men without chests."[22] That is, men (and women) without the capacities that make us truly human — virtue, imagination, humility, hope, love, etc.

Even the most convinced atheist, at the "heartfelt" level of his or her existence, usually acts as if God exists. According to the Bible, at some basic level we all *know* that God exists.[23] We can know God "through the things he has made,"[24] and also through conscience which is our innate sense of right and wrong. Through these gifts we at least vaguely know that there is a moral order in the universe (natural law). We simply cannot escape the moral categories of good and evil, right and wrong, the beautiful and the heinous. "We know God is there," writes Timothy Keller, "that is why even when we believe with all our minds that life is meaningless, we simply can't live that way. We know better."[25] But if God's existence is "known" intuitively, why do many people reject the reality of God?

---

21. The theory presented here on the evolution of a kiss has, as far as I know, absolutely no basis in evolutionary biological science. I made this up only as an example of the limits of purely rational inquiry — thinking only with the head and not also with the heart.

22. Cf. C.S. Lewis, *The Abolition of Man.*

23. Cf. Romans 1.

24. Romans 1:20.

25. Timothy Keller, *The Reason for God* (New York: Dutton, 2008), 142.

There are certainly many reasons why people reject the existence of God. We could point to the poor example of those who say they believe in God. This was succinctly captured on a bumper sticker: "God, save us from your followers!" Pascal understood this truth when he wrote more than 300 years ago: "Men never do evil so completely and cheerfully as when they do it from religious conviction."[26] Believers behaving badly is certainly a major stumbling block to faith in God.

Another reason people offer for their atheism is simply because they subjectively "feel" more comfortable without God. The atheist Michael Shermer, who is the publisher of *Skeptic Magazine*, explains why he eventually rejected the theistic option:

> ...when I moved from theism to atheism and science as a worldview I guess to be honest I just liked the people in science and the scientists and their books and, just that lifestyle and the way of living. I liked that better than the religious books, the religious people I was hanging out with, just socially it felt more comfortable to me.... If you're going to be honest it's not just reasoning your way to a position. In reality I think most of us arrive at most of our beliefs for non-rational reasons and then we justify them with these reasons after the fact.[27]

Note this: Michael Shermer rejected belief in God *not* because all the rational evidence refuted God's existence. He reached his conclusion for much more subjective, heartfelt reasons.[28] He "liked" atheism better than theism. He has faith that God does not exist.

---

26. As quoted by Daniel Taylor in *The Myth of Certainty* (Downers Grove, IL: InterVarsity, second printing 1992), 27.

27. *The Question of God: Does God Really Exist?* (PBS Home Video, 2004). See also the book by Dr. Armand M. Nicholi, Jr., *The Question of God: C.S. Lewis and Sigmund Freud Debate God, Love, Sex, and the Meaning of Life* (New York: The Free Press, 2002).

28. Allister McGrath, who holds a doctorate from Oxford in biophysics, says that most of the unbelieving scientists that he knows are atheist for many different reasons. Their scientific training did not necessarily lead

Evil and the Existence of God

God judged it better to bring good out of evil, than to allow no evil to exist. — St. Augustine

If evil exists, God exists. — St. Thomas Aquinas

There are people who simply prefer to live as if God did not exist. However, the vast majority of people believe, or want to believe, in God. Yet even for believers, when terrible things happen, we can begin to question. Why, if God is good, is there so much evil?

The problem of evil is undoubtedly the greatest obstacle to belief in God's existence. I began this chapter with a story of the suffering of a small boy. That little boy died. How can we believe in an infinitely good God in a world in which there is such horrible suffering? After combing through the objections to God's existence, St. Thomas Aquinas said that only the reality of evil is truly problematic for faith.[29] In other words, we are able with a great deal of intellectual and philosophical sophistication to defend belief in God's existence. What we're not able to prove is whether or not God gives a damn about us.

Elie Wiesel, who is a survivor of the Nazi Holocaust, tells a haunting story in his autobiographical work *Night*. Wiesel writes of the execution of three prisoners. One of those hanged was just a young boy:

> The SS seemed more preoccupied, more disturbed than usual. To hang a young boy in front of thousands of

---

them to atheism. Rather, as the sociologist Peter Berger has shown, personal, social, intellectual, and cultural factors greatly influence our personal beliefs and perceptions of reality. Cf. Timothy Keller, *The Reason for God* (New York: Dutton, 2008), 90.

29. *Summa Theologiae, 1.2.3. "Whether God Exists,"* Frederick Christian Bauerschmidt, *Holy Teaching: Introducing the Summa Theologiae of St. Thomas Aquinas* (Grand Rapids: Brazos, 2005), 50-51. See also, Peter Kreeft, *A Shorter Summa: The Essential Philosophical Passages of St. Thomas Aquinas' Summa Theologica Edited and Explained* (San Francisco: Ignatius, 1993), 53, fn 2.

spectators was no light matter. The head of the camp read the verdict. All eyes were on this child. He was lividly pale, almost calm, biting his lips. The gallows threw its shadow over him.

This time the Lagerkapo refused to act as executioner. Three SS replaced him. The three victims mounted together onto the chairs. The three necks were placed at the same moment within the nooses....

"Where is God? Where is he?" someone behind me asked. At a sign from the head of the camp, the three chairs were tipped over.[30]

After the execution, all were made to walk past those who were hanging. The two men were already dead, but the child, "being so light" was still struggling. He struggled for more than half an hour. As the boy slowly died, Elie Wiesel heard a voice of a fellow prisoner somewhere behind him asking, "Where is God now?" And Elie Wiesel heard a voice within himself which said, "Where is He? Here He is — He is hanging here on this gallows."[31]

The Christian faith points us in a similar direction. Where is God in the midst of human evil and suffering? The Christian responds, "There he is, hanging on the cross."

The Theology of the Cross (The Crucified God)

The real question is not so much God's existence. The knowledge of God is "in a general and confused way ... implanted in us by nature."[32] What we cannot know "by nature" is whether or not God loves us. The God of nature gives few clues of his

---

30. Elie Wiesel, *Night* (New York: Bantam Books, 1982), 61.

31. Ibid., 62.

32. Thomas Aquinas, *Summa Theologiae in Holy Teaching: Introducing the Summa Theologiae of St. Thomas Aquinas*, Frederick Christian Bauerschmidt (Grand Rapids: Brazos Press, 2005), 47.

love. Nature is both beautiful and deadly. How can we know God loves us? The only possible way is for God to tell us and show us. This, Christians believe, God did most powerfully through Christ on the cross.

The Christian looks at the world "cross-eyed." God "hides" himself in the suffering, weakness, and shame of the cross. Somehow, the sufferings of the whole world are caught up with, and united to, the sufferings of the crucified God. Jesus is "Immanuel", which means, "God with us." God is so intimately and truly united with Jesus that, "apart from this human being there is no God."[33]

But there's much more. We are united to God in our sufferings, but we are also united to God through the Resurrection of Christ. Therefore, just as the sufferings of Christ did not have the last word, so our suffering does not have the last word because the Crucified One is also the Risen One. Please note that last sentence. Jesus Christ is not only crucified, but he is risen!

To believe in God is to believe that his life and love are stronger than death and evil. At the Last Judgment "all the evils of human history, and every wrong will be set right."[34] Until that "last word" for which we hope is spoken, until the stench of death and the absurdity of suffering is defeated, we "are permitted to hate these things with a perfect hatred."[35] So in the lament of every evil event and all suffering, we do not see the face of God. We see the face of God's enemy.

In the Uffizi Museum located in Florence, Italy, there is a painting by Cigoli (1559-1613) entitled *St. Francis Receives*

---

33. "Solid Declaration," VIII.81 in *The Book of Concord: The Confessions of the Evangelical Lutheran Church*, Robert Kolb and Timothy Wengert, eds. (Minneapolis: Fortress Press, 2000), 631; quoting Luther's *Confession Concerning Christ's Supper* (1528).

34. Richard John Neuhaus, *American Babylon: Notes of a Christian in Exile* (New York: Basic Books, 2009), 242.

35. David B. Hart, "Tsunami and Theodicy," *First Things* (March, 2005).

the Stigmata. As many are undoubtedly aware, St. Francis was one of those rare and mystical Christians who so deeply shared in Christ's sufferings that the wounds of Christ's crucifixion actually appeared on his body — the *stigmata*. In the painting, Francis is kneeling and there is an open Bible on the ground before him. His half-closed eyes look up to heaven and his arms are open in supplication. Francis is depicted in relative darkness, but in the top right of the painting there is brilliant light. It seems fluorescent. In the light there is a dimly painted dove coming towards Francis, and superimposed on the dove is a crucifix. Rays of light coming from the dove and crucifix strike Francis. There is a look of both suffering and ecstasy on the saint's face. He shares both in the darkness of Christ's suffering, and also in the light of Christ's glory.[36]

In this painting, Cigoli masterfully captured the Christian understanding of God. Where is God when we suffer? He who hung on the cross suffers with us, through us, and we with him. The power of Christ's resurrection is at work in the suffering shared with Christ. This does not "solve" the problem of human suffering and evil, but it can help us to endure suffering without surrendering to despair and to fight against evil rather than surrendering to apathy. Perhaps any suffering can be endured, and even made fruitful, when we know that God is present with us, and within us, and that nothing ultimately can separate us from His love.[37] John Stott captures the heart of what is at stake in this discussion: "I could never myself believe in God, if it were not for the cross.... In the real world of pain, how could one worship a God who was immune to it?"[38]

The crucified God is not immune to our pain, but shares it. Ultimately, Jesus is the best reason not only to believe in God, but also to love him.

---

36. I Peter 4:13.

37. Romans 8:28.

38. John R.W. Stott, *The Cross of Christ* (Downers Grove, IL: InterVarsity Press, 1986), 335.

Trusting the Triune God

*Go and make disciples of all nations, baptizing them
in the name of the Father, and of the Son, and of the
Holy Spirit, and teaching them to obey everything I have
commanded you. And surely I am with you, to the very
end of the age.* — Matthew 28:19-20

There is one other essential doctrine that must be discussed,
and that is the Christian confession that God is "Triune." This
means, that God is eternally One and yet mysteriously Three:
"Father, Son, and Holy Spirit."

The division between monotheistic believers is nowhere
more evident than when discussing the doctrine of the Holy
Trinity. The Muslim writer Reza Aslan, says that Islam considers the doctrine of the Holy Trinity to be one of the "intolerable heretical innovations created by ignorance and error."[39]
Reza Aslan quotes the Quran: "God is eternal. He has neither
begotten anyone, nor is he begotten of anyone" (*Sura* 112:
1-3). Then Reza Aslan adds this commentary:

> ...this verse, and the many others like it in the Quran, is
> in no way a condemnation of Christianity *per se* but of
> Imperial Byzantine (Trinitarian) Orthodoxy.... What the
> Quran does not accept ... is the belief of those Ortho-
> dox Trinitarians who argued that Jesus was *himself* God.
> These Christians Muhammad did not even consider to
> be Peoples of the Book.[40]

According to Reza Aslan, Muhammad believed that these
"Orthodox Trinitarian" Christians had "corrupted the original message of Jesus."[41] These Orthodox Christians are even
called "unbelievers" in the Quran: "It is the unbeliever who
says, 'God is the third of the trinity'"(*Sura* 5:73). This is, of

---

39. Reza Aslan, *No god but God* (New York: Random House, 2005/2006),
    101.

40. Ibid., 101-102.

41. Ibid., 102.

course, a misunderstanding of the doctrine of the Holy Trinity. No traditional "orthodox" Christian theologian would ever say that each Person of the Trinity comprises a third of God. Our theological disagreement over this doctrine may possibly be one of those cases in which what is called disagreement is really only confusion.[42] While Christians and Muslims (or Jews) may never fully agree on the doctrine of the Trinity, hopefully greater mutual understanding may dull the edge to some of our most divisive theological differences.[43]

It should be noted that Trinitarian doctrine arose very early in the life of the Church as Christians reflected on the filial relationship between God and the eternal Word (*logos*) incarnate in Jesus. This theological reflection is part of the New Testament itself (cf. Matthew 28:19; John 1:1ff. and many other passages). Reza Alan's incorrect (yet confident) assertion that the Gospels were "written by many different writers over hundreds of years," is simply wrong (compare chapter 3). So what exactly do Christians believe? What is the doctrine of the Holy Trinity?

I began this chapter trying to show that God is always infinitely greater than we can think or imagine. The doctrine of the Trinity arose in the Church as a way to talk about the God who, according to the biblical story, is revealed as the Father who creates, the Son who suffered to redeem us, and the Spirit who sanctifies and sustains us. This is not a mathematical problem to be solved, but a mystery to be lived and a relationship in which we are now joined, and will be eternally joined in heaven. The beauty of this doctrine lies in the fact that it took centuries of thought, sifting through the Scriptures, praying for guidance, arguments and counterarguments; until a catholic

---

42. Cf. Richard John Neuhaus article, "A University of a Particular Kind," *First Things* 172 (April, 2007), 34.

43. Perhaps one possible path to greater understanding may be along the lines of the traditionalist Muslim's understanding of the Quran as God's "eternal and uncreated" Word. A Word that, according to Muslims, became a book — the Quran. What Muslims believe about a Book, Christians believe about a Person — Jesus Christ.

consensus was reached. Pope Emeritus Benedict XVI high-lights our inability to express logically the mystery of the doctrine of the Holy Trinity:

> Every one of the main basic concepts in the doctrine of the Trinity was condemned at one time or another; they were all adopted only after the frustration of a condemnation; they are accepted only so inasmuch as they are at the same time branded as unusable and admitted *only as poor stammering utterances* — and no more (emphasis added).[44]

We Christians stammer a great and wonderful mystery when we confess: "I believe in God the Father, Son, and Holy Spirit." This should not surprise us. God is always wholly Other than we can conceive.

---

44. Joseph Cardinal Ratzinger, *Introduction to Christianity*, trans. J.R. Foster (San Francisco: Ignatius Press, 2004), 172.

Questions for Discussion

1. Why do you believe in God? Can God's existence be proven by reason alone?

2. If you could ask God one question, what would it be?

3. Someone once said that, "A saint is a person who makes it easier to believe in God." Who are the saints in your life?

4. The Russian writer Fyodor Dostoevsky once said, "If there is no God, then everything is permissible." What did he mean?

5. What does Jesus' suffering on the cross tell us about God?

6. Christians believe that God revealed Himself to us as Father, Son, and Holy Spirit; what does this tell us about God? Is it difficult for you to think of God as a Holy Trinity? What would you say to someone who said that Christians believe in three gods?

7. The 17th century Christian, Blaise Pascal once said that, "Men never do evil more willingly than when they do it from religious conviction." That is, when we believe that God is on our side. How is this a danger for religious people today?

Chapter 2
Is the Universe Friendly?
The Goodness of God

Poor boys and pilgrims with families and we are going to Graceland. My traveling companion is nine years old. He is the child of my first marriage, but I've reason to believe we both will be received in Graceland. — Paul Simon

The law indeed was given through Moses; grace and truth came through Jesus Christ. — John 1:17

Grace is everywhere.... — Georges Bernanos

Cheap grace means the justification of the sin without the justification of the sinner. — Dietrich Bonhoeffer

Quick story: One day the great Christian thinker C.S. Lewis came across a group of his Oxford peers discussing religion. They were arguing whether or not there was one, unique belief that separated Christianity from other religions. When Lewis entered the room he asked, "What's the rumpus about?" The scholars looked up and said, "There's Jack, he'll be able to help us." So they asked Lewis if he thought there was anything truly unique about Christianity. Didn't all religions tell tales of incarnations and resurrections? And didn't all religions teach basically the same moral premises? What separates Christianity from other religions? Were there any substantial differences among them? Weren't they all teaching people to live good lives? So when Lewis was asked his opinion he responded: "Oh, that's easy, it's grace."

C.S. Lewis was right. The best, the truest, and the most unique thing about Christianity is grace. Ultimately, it all boils down to whether or not grace is real. Everything else is detail. The heart of the Christian faith centers on the belief in a God of grace. Grace is the sun in the theological solar system of Christianity. To understand the Christian faith we *must* understand grace. Remove grace from Christianity and we might as well spend more time at the movies or the mall. "Grace," writes Philip Yancey, "contains the essence of the gospel as a drop of water contains the image of the sun."[45] The essence of a thing is the essential truth of it. Grace contains the essence of the truth of Christianity.

What is grace? Traditionally, Christians have spoken of two kinds of grace — "common and special." Common grace is God's goodness experienced by everyone in a "common" or "general" way. Earlier, I mentioned Stephen Hawking. He's an atheist, but God graced him with a profound intellect. Likewise, God makes his sun rise and shine on sinners and saints. The just and the unjust both enjoy good things.[46] The believer and the unbeliever enjoy health, friendship, stable government, and all the beauty of nature. These gifts are the common work of God's grace. It's not only Christians who "say grace" before a meal. Other religions faiths have the same offering of thanks for the common God-given gifts.

Christians also speak of "special" or "sanctifying" grace. This is the grace which works faith, hope, and love in us. The Roman Catholic Church understands grace as a power sacramentally "infused" (think of a sponge soaking up water) enabling us, in cooperation with God, to be transformed into saints. This is what is called *sanctification*. We are saved by God's grace. We can't be saved by our own moral efforts or intellectual gifts.

---

45. Philip Yancey, *What's So Amazing About Grace* (Grand Rapids: Zondervan, 1997), 13.

46. Matthew 5:45.

The *Catechism of the Catholic Church* states that grace is "the *free and undeserved help* that God gives us to respond to his call to become children of God." Grace is God's active presence and power in us that helps us, at least partially, to become the people God has called us to be. God graciously welcomes and receives sinners *in order to transform them into saints*. God's grace is a power that enables us to live lives of faith, hope, and love. And please note, God's grace is not earned. God does not hold back waiting for us to make the first move. God takes the initiative and comes to us and works within us to heal the damage caused by sin and thereby perfecting our fallen nature. As St. Thomas Aquinas so famously stated, grace "does not destroy nature but perfects it."[47] Every human being is a potential Masterpiece.

Many Protestants use the word grace in a "forensic" or legal sense. Grace is not so much understood as a power to transform us, but rather as the goodness of God to *pardon* us. Grace is shorthand for God's underserved forgiveness of our sins for the sake of Jesus Christ. It is still popular to hear Protestants define grace as: God's Riches At Christ's Expense (**GRACE**). God is gracious because Christ paid the penalty for our sin, and bore God's judgment against sin *for us. Since* God in Christ has done this for us, *therefore* ethical imperatives to be transformed, or sanctified, follow.[48]

So which is correct? What is grace? Is grace a power that transforms us from sinner to saint? Or is grace just getting off the hook? Both say something true, but neither captures the fullness of the word. Grace is simply too big of a truth to be so easily tamed.

---

47. *Summa Theologiae* 1.1.8, 5.3.1, etc. and *Summa Contra Gentiles* 3.148.2.

48. Many have noted that the strong emphasis upon forensic justification among some Protestants has, at times, left the ethical imperatives neglected. Isn't there, as Robert Benne notes, an "antinomian whiff to this account of justification by grace?" (cf. *Ordinary Saints*, Minneapolis: Fortress, 2003), 97-98.

Grace is *everything*— common or special — that God does for us. It's true that God remains *hidden*, but behind the scenes grace is at work. Through the earth and the farmer who works the earth, God feeds us. We don't see God at work. He's hidden. But if God stopped creating, then we'd starve.

Or, think of Jesus on the cross. God hid Himself in a cruel and shameful death. It certainly did not look like God was at work. It's certainly not what we usually expect God to look like. It looked like God was *MIA* — *missing in action.* Yet, the cross was God's greatest work of saving grace.[49]

Another story is helpful here.

Is the Universe Friendly?

A reporter once asked Albert Einstein what he thought to be the most important question a person could ask. With barely a pause Einstein responded, "Whether the universe is friendly or not."[50] At the core of the Christian faith is the assertion that ultimately life in this universe is friendly because God is graciously *for us.* The life we so often experience as struggle and heartache and suffering (a life in which God may even seem to be absent) is ultimately good and gracious and beautiful *because* God is at work to save us. To put it simply, grace is the Good News that God wants to be our Friend.[51] And very importantly, God does not want to befriend only the most popular, successful, affluent, and beautiful people. God desires to befriend moral and spiritual failures too.[52]

Of course, this is difficult to accept. The world does not operate by grace. The world operates on the principle of self-generated success and failure. We all earn our way in life. We

---

49. We'll look carefully at the significance of the cross in chapter 4.
50. Jeffrey G. Sobosan, *Romancing the Universe: Theology, Science, and Cosmology* (Grand Rapids: Eerdmans, 1999), 12.
51. John 14:14-15.
52. cf. Luke 15:1ff.

earn respect. We *earn* a living. We *earn* praise or punishment. Justice is getting what we deserve. The "saved" are the successful. Employees work to attract positive notice, earn merit, receive promotions, and increase their pay. Students strive to attract the interest of the best colleges and universities. High school athletes struggle to attract the notice of college scouts. All of us spend a great deal of time and energy trying to attract positive attention and deflect negative attention. It's the way the world works (and in many ways how it *must* work). It's also why so many people feel stressed, burned out, depressed, and insecure. What if I'm not smart enough? Good enough? Attractive enough? Does it mean that I am a total failure if someone else gets the promotion I expected? I deserved? If the only salvation is success, then the worst thing in life is to fail.

But sooner or later, no matter how hard we try, we discover that some people are simply more "attractive" and more "successful" than we are. The *Sports Illustrated* swimsuit edition is not a bestseller because the women in it are unattractive. When the average female compares herself to the photographically-enhanced vision of beauty in the swimsuit edition, or the average male to the stud on the cover of *GQ*, we naturally feel (and look) like failures.

It's a cutthroat world in which there are winners and losers. The goal for many is to outdo the competition and get to the top by any means necessary. As the old saying has it: "To win isn't everything, it's the only thing." It's a "meritocracy."[53] We merit our way into the world's acceptance by our looks, our position, our power, and our wealth. This is how the world works, but this is *not* how God works.

Grace is God's heart revealed. Grace tells us that God is attracted to us *not* because of our own goodness, physical beauty, holiness, accomplishments, or wealth. God is attracted to us because *God* is good. This is the central and foundational truth of the Christian faith. But is it too good to be true?

---

53. Daniel B. Clendenin, journeywithjesus.net, September 21, 2008.

Don't we all harbor the suspicion that the Universe is ultimately cold, uncaring, and very unfriendly? Stop and think about the manifold horrors and tragedies which regularly happen on any given day, and we may begin to wonder whether God is our Friend or our Enemy. What if God is not *for us*, but *against us?*

Living in a Graceless World?

I've often heard people ask, "If God is as gracious and loving as you say, then why does He let such evil things happen in this world?" The world is often a graceless wilderness. Millions of people lack the basic necessities of life, and our inhumanity against each other goes on and on unchecked by God. Disease and death are rampant. How can anyone say that God is gracious and can be trusted?

A few years ago I was on a plane. I was wearing a clerical collar. This often sparks interest. So, sitting next to me there was man about my age and we struck up a conversation. Over the next hour and a half I learned that he had recently buried his 17-year-old son. His son had just gotten a driver's license, borrowed the car, and picked up his best friend. There was an accident. His son's best friend was killed. Six months later, in his bedroom, unable to bear the guilt, the son took a gun and killed himself. God seemed to be against this man. It was a long flight.

I'm reminded of a story about St. Teresa of Avila. One night she and a group of other nuns were traveling. It was in the middle of a storm. She was wet, cold, and filled with fear, dread, and depression, so she asked God why this was happening. And God spoke to her: "Teresa, do not be dismayed. I treat all my friends like this." To which the witty Saint responded: "Perhaps that's why you have so few."

Undoubtedly one of God's greatest miracles is that he sustains faith in a world that often seems graceless, devoid of divine friendship. Yet, God *somehow* still has friends. Here's a story told by Phillip Yancey about a man named Douglas who had more than his share of "unfriendly" experiences in life, yet remained God's friend.

44

Douglas' troubles began when his wife found a lump on her breast. After a biopsy, the lump was found to be malignant and she began a course of chemotherapy that caused the usual and horrible side effects. One afternoon while they were going through the struggle with cancer, Douglas was driving with his wife and their 12-year-old daughter when they were suddenly struck by a drunk driver. His wife and daughter were shaken, but not badly injured. Douglas sustained a severe, massive head injury that left him permanently disabled. In the aftermath, he began to suffer terrible headaches. He could no longer focus his mind for serious study. He was a lover of books, but now he was limited to listening to recorded books on tape. After all this, you would think Douglas would either laugh in your face or be angered by the suggestion that God is gracious. Philip Yancey interviewed Douglas and asked him, "Could you tell me about your own disappointment with God." And Douglas said, "To tell you the truth, Philip, I didn't feel any disappointment." At first, Philip Yancey found this response to be rather unbelievable. When asked, after all he had endured, why he was not disappointed with God, Douglas said:

The reason is this. I learned, first through my wife's illness and then especially through the accident, not to confuse God with life. I'm no stoic. I am as upset about what happened to me as anyone could be. I feel free to curse the unfairness of life and to vent all my grief and anger. But I believe God feels the same way about that accident - grieved and angry. I don't blame him for what happened.... I have learned to see beyond the physical reality in this world to the spiritual reality. We tend to think, 'Life should be fair because God is fair.' But God is not life. And if I confuse God with the physical reality of life — by expecting constant good health, for example — then I set myself up for a crashing disappointment.[54]

God is not life. What does that mean? It means that the intricate web of human suffering is not woven directly by God.

---

54. Philip Yancey, *Disappointment with God: Three Questions no One Asks Aloud* (Grand Rapids: Zondervan, 1988), 183.

God did not *cause* the drunk driver to crash into Douglas' car. God didn't steer the car in which that young man was killed, or pull the trigger. There is free will.

However, no matter how hard we "will" it, we can't extricate ourselves from the web of sin and suffering in which we are caught. I wish, *really wish*, I could tell people that if they only tried a little harder or believed a little stronger or loved a little longer (song lyrics?) then we could free ourselves from our predicament. If only we could all be little engines that could and just practice the power of positive thinking. Then there would be no more drunk drivers and teenagers would be naturally cautious. But, it ain't gonna happen.

The truth is that we are all caught in an intricate web of human actions and inactions freely chosen. So we can freely choose to start unnecessary wars, kill millions of unborn children, carelessly destroy the environment, watch porn, and drive drunk. Whoopie! All our human effort fails to move us morally forward.

One would think that after all these years we might begin to figure out that free will might not be the answer, but the problem. Drunk drivers act freely. No one is forcing them to drive. And what about young, inexperienced drivers? Most of us wanted to drive so that we could be free and go where we wanted to go and do what we wanted to do. Driving gives us a form of freedom. Yet, as long as we are ensnared in the web of sin, exercising our free will is like a car stuck in the mud. The faster the wheels spin the deeper we sink. It's going nowhere. Nothing changes for the better.

The story of Adam and Eve is meant to give expression to our human situation. How did we get into such a mess? St. Paul writes that the first strand woven in the web of sin in which we are all ensnared started with Adam.[55] Adam and Eve wanted freedom from the constraints God placed upon them. Maybe God just wanted all that delicious forbidden fruit for himself?

---

55. Romans 5:12ff.

Who does he think he is? God? Friendship was broken. Free at last! Or so we think.

Adam is us. That's right. He's the head of the human race. The story of Adam isn't about someone else who lived a long time ago in a land far away. It's a story that goes on and on. Each time we exercise our free will and gobble down the forbidden fruit, we dig ourselves deeper into the mess. Who are you to tell me what to eat? Or how to live? Or what to do? I'm free! Really?

Think of it like playing a musical instrument. I play guitar and am better than average. It took a lot of time, discipline, and practice. Now I can play some things *freely and gracefully*. My fingers no longer feel awkward and clumsy when forming a chord. Freedom is like playing beautiful music. It doesn't happen apart from discipline or just because we *will* it.

The primary reason we live in such a graceless world is because we keep choosing freedom apart from God. This is our bondage: untrained and unskilled musicians playing the symphony of life with no Conductor. Or perhaps the *wrong* conductor. Either way, life begins to sound like a John Cage concert. His compositions are mostly long periods of silence punctuated by a few dissonant notes. There's no beauty to it.

To make matters worse, we're stuck in this together. We're all members of the same out-of-tune and off-beat orchestra. We need a new Conductor. We need a new head, a new Adam. We need to be connected to the mind of Christ the Conductor. Then we begin to learn to live and play freely *and* beautifully.

If God Be for Us

The bad news is that we can't free ourselves. The good news is that God acts to free us. This is grace. By grace we're set free to trust God who is at work causing "all things to work together for the good of those who love Him."[56] When we experience

---

56. Romans 8:28.

pain and suffering in this life, when our worst nightmare comes true, God is still at work. God's grace comes to us in real, tangible ways. There are means of grace like sacraments, but God also comes to us in surprising and unexpected ways. While not necessarily taking the suffering away, grace enables us to endure it without surrendering to despair. God still has friends. Again, in this world, that alone is a miracle.

The most important question we must ask ourselves is not "why" terrible things happen to people. Rather, we must ask "if" these terrible things are the *ultimate* things in life. Or, to echo Einstein, "Is the Universe ultimately friendly?" Is God still gracious and good when life turns bad? The answer proposed by the Christian faith is: "Yes, in Christ we know that God is always and forever *for us* even when life turns against us."

Grace is the unique heart of the Christian faith.

Questions for Discussion

1. How would you define grace?

2 Have you ever had a time in your life when you experienced God's grace?

3. Read II Corinthians 12:7-9. Paul writes about a mysterious "thorn in the flesh." He asked God to take this away, but God would not do so. What does God tell Paul about grace? Do you have "thorns" in your life you want God to remove? If so, what are they? How has God's grace given you strength?

3. Have you ever experienced grace as the power of forgiveness? Can you tell about it?

4. What are you most grateful for?

5. Can you think of a time in which a person showed you grace? Can you think about a time in which someone was ungracious?

6. What does it mean to do something *gracefully?* Dance? Music? Athletics?

7. Remember what Douglas learned through his personal tragedies that we must not "confuse God with life." Now, think of a tragic experience in your life or the life of someone you know. How are God and life sometimes confused?

8. Do you believe that the universe is ultimately friendly?

Chapter 3
Does God Speak Today?
The Written Word of God

The Bible provides the master code for reality. — R.R. Reno

God's Word is a living dialogue between God and humanity. — Charles J. Chaput, O.F.M.

The Bible is not first of all a book of moral truth. I would call it instead a book of truth about the way life is. Those strange old scriptures present life as having been ordered in a certain way, with certain laws as inextricably built into it as the law of gravity is built into the physical universe. When Jesus says that whoever would save his life will lose it and whoever loses his life will save it, surely he is not making a statement about how, morally speaking, life ought to be. Rather, he is making a statement about how life is. — Frederick Buechner

I wasn't raised in the Church. We weren't even C&E (Christmas and Easter) Christians. My interest in the Bible was stirred when I was about 17 years old. Some friends invited me to go to a Christian concert. The music was excellent, and afterward a young and dynamic pastor spoke. Then, he invited anyone who was interested to come forward for prayer. I remember sitting there on the floor feeling awkward and embarrassed, but also wanting to have the same certainty of faith that the pastor seemed to have. Suddenly, a brave and very attractive young lady who was sitting near me, got up and went forward. To this day I do not know if it was the Spirit or the flesh that caused me to overcome my embarrassment, but forward I went following in the wake of that lovely young woman.

In the ensuing talk with the pastor, I asked how a person could "get" faith. I wanted to believe, but how could we "know" that the Bible and the Christian faith were true? I wanted some proof so that I *could* believe.

The pastor responded by asking me to begin reading the Bible and prayerfully ask God to speak to me. He challenged me to do this for three weeks. He said that if the ember of faith was not sparked during this time I should come back and he would pray for me every day for three weeks. So I began to read the Bible. Every day I read it and every day I prayed. I started with the gospels, and moved to the writings of Paul. I saw no visions and heard no voices, but something or Someone hooked me.

I can almost hear the questions coming to mind in some readers. Converts to various religions have gotten hooked on a book, but this does not necessarily make the book true. For example, I am convinced that the *Book of Mormon* is a fabrication of an overly active religious imagination. However, many people swear by it and claim that God has spoken to them through it. My point is that I was first hooked by the Bible (or by God through the Bible), and this started me on a quest to understand the Bible. Was it true? Or was it the product of many overly active religious imaginations?

So I continued to read and study the Bible and attend church. In the process, I discovered a whole community of people who were asking many of the same questions that I had. So I joined that conversation, and was "surprised by faith." God sneaked up on me through the Scriptures and I found myself, more or less, a believer. At the same time, my desire for knowledge led me to study and ultimately to discover that there were some things about the Bible that we could, with various degrees of certainty, *know*.

Bible 101

Pick up a Bible. You hold in your hands a small library of ancient documents. The earliest documents are the written record of oral traditions going back about 4,000 years. The Old Testament (or Hebrew Scriptures) is a compilation of early writings stitched together by ancient Hebrew priests and prophets.[57] It tells the sacred story of the people of Israel. A sacred story, but it's not always a pretty one. The people who, under the providential guidance of God, preserved these writings for us did not spare us from stories of failure and faithlessness. More often than not, the Jewish people failed to walk in the "statutes and ordinances" of the LORD. The kings of Israel were usually corrupt and the Temple priests complicit. It's a dismally repeating cycle of apostasy, warning, judgment, repentance, restoration; then back to apostasy.

With no end in sight to this ongoing mess, there emerged among those ancient Jews a hope that the cycle of sin would be permanently broken. Israel would become and remain faithful. To make this happen, God would send an ideal, true, faithful King — the Messiah. This Messiah would spring from the "root of Jesse."[58] That is, from the lineage of King David. This new King would unite people to himself so that "all the nations" would be drawn to the God of Israel and learn to live in peace — *shalom*.[59]

---

57. Scholars have tried to understand the historical process of this "stitching together" of the Old Testament. One prominent theory seeking to understand how this happened is called the "documentary hypothesis" or "source theory" made famous by a German scholar, Julius Wellhausen (1844-1914). He isolated various sources of the Old Testament which he labeled J, E, P, and D. These letters represent various strains of traditions within the Old Testament: J = Jahwist, E = Elohist, P = Priestly, and D = Deuteronomist. For a fuller discussion on this topic see John Bright, *A History of Israel* (Philadelphia: The Westminster Press, 1981), 68ff. Recently, this theory has come under suspicion. It is a "theory," not a fact.

58. Isaiah 11:1.

59. Isaiah 2.

At the same time, there were hints that not all would be so peachy. The hope for Messiah was merged with another figure, *the suffering servant*. The Prophet Isaiah said of him:

> He was despised and rejected by men; a man of sorrows, and acquainted with grief; and as one from whom men hide their faces he was despised, and we esteemed him not ... we esteemed him stricken, smitten by God, and afflicted. But he was pierced for our transgressions, he was crushed for our iniquities; upon him was the chastisement that brought us peace (*shalom*).[60]

Early Christians believed that Jesus was both Messiah (Christ) *and* suffering servant. He made sense of both Israel's hope that the cycle of faithlessness would be broken, and the fact that the person who broke the cycle would suffer in the process. It is a fool's errand to believe that God can be served without suffering.

The New Testament was written by those who believed in Jesus — Messiah and Suffering Servant of the LORD — and wanted others to believe in him too. Whereas the Old Testament is the work of centuries, the entire New Testament was written within about fifty years, from approximately 50-100 A.D. The two testaments, or covenants, are intimately linked. They bear witness to the work of the same God. Together they tell the "history of salvation."

Not a Book, but a Library

Since the Bible is a library of ancient documents, it contains many *genres* (kinds) of writings: myth, legend, poetry, history, proverb, parable, letters, and more. It has a big cast of characters.

> [It's] a big book, full of big stories with big characters. They have big ideas (not least about themselves) and make big mistakes. It's about God and greed and grace; about life, lust, laughter, and loneliness. It's about birth,

---

60. Cf. Isaiah 53:3-5.

54

beginnings, and betrayal, about siblings, squabbles, and sex; about power and prayer and prison and passion. And that's only Genesis.[61]

The Bible was written by real people. It was not dictated directly by angels as were, supposedly, the *Book of Mormon* and the Islamic Qu'ran.[62] The Bible is a library of historical documents reflecting the political and cultural climate of the ancient Near Middle East from about 1800 B.C. to 100 A.D. The writers were people of their own times and places. Yet, their writings also reflect truths that are eternal and which speak to people of all times and places. God continues to speak through these old books and stories. The Bible *is* the written Word of God. Therefore it does what God wants it to do. It sheds the Light of God's Truth into the darkness of this world and draws us to that Light.

Because the Bible Says So?

There was a time in our society when what the Bible said was an important question. People respected the Bible (or at least pretended to do so). "The Bible says" had some cultural clout. Things have changed. Today, if you are in a public meeting discussing some important issue and defend your position with "the Bible says," you will be labeled a fool, a fundamentalist, or a fanatic — probably all three. Bible-thumpers are not thought of kindly — and for good reason.

In the Church things are quite different. By and large, Christians still care about what the Bible says. We care because the Bible contains the story of our faith. It is God's Word, the book of the Church which contains the story not only of the Church, but of the whole creation. In broad outline it is a "meta-

61. N.T. Wright, *Simply Christian: Why Christianity Makes Sense* (San Francisco: Harper, 2006), 173.

62. Galatians 1:8: "If we or an angel from heaven should preach to you a gospel contrary to the one we preached to you, let him be accursed."

narrative," a Grand Story, the Truest Story ever told, which unites, interprets, and gives meaning to all our sundry personal stories. Christians have been reading the Bible, meditating on it, studying it, and preaching on it for a very long time. Christians believe that God speaks to us through the Bible. Again, it is inspired by God. At the very least, the divine inspiration of the Bible means that it is not a product of chance or a mere happenstance collection of ancient religious documents. The Bible is a divine gift given to us through human hands.

Obviously this inevitably leads to some tension between those who revere the Bible and those who don't. We see the same tension between those who revere the Islamic Qu'ran and those who don't. But, it also leads to a lot of tension among the various groups of Christians who *do* accept the Bible's authority. Christians don't always agree on exactly how to interpret the sacred page.

Sola Scriptura?

During the 16th century Protestant Reformation the authority of the Bible took on particular significance. Protestant Christians thought that all Church traditions should be accepted or rejected depending upon whether or not they could be squared with the Bible. They called this *sola scriptura* (*scripture alone*):

> We believe, teach, and confess that the only rule and guiding principle according to which all teachings and teachers are to be evaluated and judged are the prophetic and apostolic writings of the Old and New Testaments alone.[63]

In keeping with the doctrine of sola scriptura, Protestants also emphasized the *perspicuity of Scripture*. This is the belief that the Bible's teachings (and thus God's will) can be clearly un-

---

63. *The Formula of Concord, The Epitome, 1. The Book of Concord: The Confessions of the Evangelical Lutheran Church*, eds. Robert Kolb and Timothy J. Wengert (Minneapolis: Fortress, 2000), 486.

derstood without reference to a higher human authority to help us understand it — like the Roman Catholic Church. "Scripture," as Protestants have historically taught, "interprets Scripture." In other words, all we need to do is read the Bible and ask the Holy Spirit to help us understand and interpret it.

Martin Luther famously translated the Bible into German. He gave the people God's Word to read for themselves. As someone once said, "Luther made the Holy Spirit speak German." Anyone with an open and honest heart and mind could read it and would reach the same conclusions as Luther. Or so it was assumed.

Unfortunately, even with the Holy Spirit, the Bible proved to be open to many competing interpretations. The Church divided, "splintered" would be more accurate. Each group claimed to understand God's word more correctly than the others. The Bible proved not as clear as many thought.[64]

Today Christians are probably more divided than ever over issues concerning *the authority of the Bible.* There are splits, schisms, separations, and even a few denominational divorces. Among contemporary Protestants this is most noticeable over issues of human sexuality. What, for example, does the Bible say about homosexuality? Ask two Christians and you'll probably get three opinions. We'll look at the thorny issue of homosexuality later. Right now I want us to understand just how terribly divided Christians are over some issues. These divisions are primarily centered on disagreements over the authority and interpretation of the Bible.

So, how should we read and interpret the Bible? What are some general rules of thumb to help us understand it? There are, I believe, three things to always keep in mind as we seek

---

64. For a particularly insightful critique of the concept of the perspicuity of Scripture see Brad Gregory, *The Unintended Reformation: How a Religious Revolution Secularized Society* (Cambridge/London: The Belknap Press of Harvard University Press, 2012), especially chapter 2, "Relativizing Doctrines," 74-128.

to understand the Bible. I'll then mention a fourth specifically Lutheran aid to understanding Scripture, but here are three rules-of-thumb.

Three Rules-of-Thumb for Understanding the Bible

First, we should read the Bible through the lens of a "rule of faith" (*regula fidei*). The "rule of thumb" is "the rule of faith." The rule of faith is summarized in the Apostles and Nicene Creeds. The importance of these creeds was mentioned in the introduction.

There is always the tendency, especially in our individualistic "sez who" culture, to read the Bible asking only what it means "to me." The problem is that what the Bible means *to me* may not be what the Bible means *at all*. For example, it's rather common to hear someone say, "*I think* that the visions of Ezekiel in the Old Testament were ancient attempts to describe UFOs."[65] Now, I tend to believe in UFOs and find the possibility of a close encounter with *friendly* aliens rather appealing. However, to interpret Ezekiel's visions as such a close encounter is to move from the truly sublime to the truly ridiculous. Ezekiel's experiences bear witness to a close encounter with God which is infinitely more interesting (and entertaining) than an encounter with ancient astronauts.

The Bible must be read *with* the Church, not *against* the Church; and the Church has given us a *rule of faith*. Reading the Bible through a rule of faith helps us to separate what is most important in the Bible from what is of secondary (or less) importance. For example, the creeds tell us that God created everything. So, we confess, "I believe in God the Father Almighty creator of heaven and earth."

You, whoever you are who happen to be reading this, are not an evolutionary accident. Life is a gift, and God is the Giver.

---

65. Cf. Ezekiel 1 and the bizarre interpretations given by Erich Van Daeniken, in *Chariots of the Gods?*

It is of secondary importance "how" God created. The vast majority of scientists say that it took billions of years. But however it happened, and however long it took, the rule of faith confesses that God created. What the rule of faith "rules" out is atheism, the belief that the Universe has no Creator.

The creeds also point us to *the* central and unique truth of Christian faith: Jesus Christ rose from the dead. He "suffered... was crucified, died and was buried ... and on the third day rose again." What could be more important?

St. Paul wrote to the early Christians in Corinth that he had given to them "as of first importance" that Christ died for our sins, and that he rose again from the dead.[66] If Jesus is dead then nothing in the Bible is of any vital importance to anyone. But, if Jesus did rise from the dead, then finding out who he was, what he said, and conforming our lives to those truths is vitally, incredibly, extremely important.

The point to remember is that the creeds help us to keep first things first. Some Christians ponder the End Times and the Second Coming of Christ. They have grandiose ideas about the events which will proceed the end of the world, and write bestselling books making millions of dollars to put in bank accounts to secure their place in a world which is soon to end. Hmm? Entire Christian denominations are divided over these issues. The creeds keep it simple: "He will come again to judge the living and the dead." That's enough for us know. The rest is pious speculation.

A second rule-of-thumb: catholic Christians (those who share in the cumulative consent of faith) are in full agreement that Jesus Christ as he is presented in the Bible is the central truth of Scripture. The Book of Hebrews in the New Testament says, "Long ago God spoke to our ancestors in many and various ways by the prophets, but in these last days he has spoken to us by a Son."[67] The "last days" began with the advent of Christ.

---

66. I Corinthians 15.

67. Hebrews 1:1-2.

In an important sense, for Christians Jesus Christ "is" the interpretation of the Bible. God's word, his message, was enfleshed in a particular human life. All Scripture ultimately points to him and is fulfilled by him. As St. Paul wrote, "In the *fullness of time* God sent his son." When the moment was ripe, Mary conceived a son. The rest is his story.

When we read the Bible, we should always keep Jesus, his life, his teachings, his death, and his Resurrection in the forefront of our minds. To give one example, Jesus' love for the outcast is clearly portrayed in the gospels. His love for these unfortunates often conflicted with some other parts of the Bible which seemed to say that outcasts must clean up their act before God would accept them. Jesus, while *clearly* wanting people to clean up their acts in repentance, preached a message of forgiveness, acceptance, second chances, and new beginnings. This rubbed some of the religious leaders of his day the wrong way. They were old school: "Get-your-act-together-and-clean-yourself-up" before you come to God.

Nowhere is this tension seen more clearly than in the story of the woman caught "in the very act" of adultery.[68] Let your imagination run wild. The Old Testament Law (which is in the Bible!) said that such a woman should be stoned to death. God had specifically forbidden adultery. Adultery was wrong — and still is. The religious leaders of Jesus' day stood close, watching to see what he would do. Would he disregard the Scriptures and approve of adultery thus proving himself to be against God? A false Prophet? They thought they had him.

Everyone was waiting for his answer. He knelt down and began to write with his finger in the dirt. What he wrote is unknown. Then he stood up and said, "Okay, stone her. But let the person who is without sin cast the first stone." Then, beginning with the oldest, they all dropped their stones and sneaked off in embarrassed silence. Jesus turned to the woman

---

68. John 8:1-11.

and said, "Did no one condemn you? Neither do I condemn you. Go and sin no more."

In a few sentences Jesus silences both the unrighteous and the self-righteous. To the unrighteous, he says: "Go and sin no more." To the self-righteous: "Let him who is without sin cast the first stone." Beautiful!

Full disclosure: it is true that the story about Jesus forgiving the woman caught in adultery (John 8) is *not* found in the best ancient manuscripts of John. At some point, this story existed independently and was inserted. Does this make the story untrue? A fabrication? No, not at all. It makes it a story which the Church judged to be consistent with what Jesus actually said and did. Think of it like the stories our families tell of our parents or grandparents. We've all heard stories told by one family member which are unknown to other family members even when they grew up in the same house. Interestingly, the Gospel of John is the only gospel in which this story is told. It ends with these words:

> There are many other things which Jesus did. Were every one of them to be written, I suppose that the world itself could not contain the books that would be written (John 21:25).

Jesus is just too big to fit into any book.

The third rule-of-thumb that helps us understand and interpret the Bible is that we must use our brains. Reason is a God-given gift. No one should ever be asked to stop thinking and just believe because "*the Bible says so!*"

Of course, we use our intellects *prayerfully*. We read the Scriptures with intellectual and spiritual openness and attentiveness to God, but questions are encouraged. To question is *not* a sign of a lack of faith, but often a sign of the birth of faith. If the Bible truly is God's Word, then we need to use our intellects to help us hear, understand, and obey it. This is one way we can worship God with our *minds*.

However, let's face it, there's some wild stuff in there. As a pastor I preach regularly on the Bible. What do I say about a talking snake, seas miraculously parting, God appearing in a burning bush, healings, exorcisms, walking on water, and people being raised from the dead?

There's a lot in the Bible that is not part of our everyday experience. When was the last time you saw someone being raised from the dead? Maybe we should only believe the parts that are consistent with our experience and understanding? Thomas Jefferson famously did this when he cut out all the parts of the Bible that didn't square with his enlightened worldview. When he was finished, there wasn't much left. How do we respond? "Don't ask questions"?

To begin, we must admit that the people who wrote the Bible knew little or nothing about things like evolution, cosmology, genetics, or geology. God did not miraculously provide the writers of the Bible with scientific knowledge. So we cannot read the Bible as a scientific text book. A person who wants to be a surgeon will gain little knowledge of anatomy by studying the Bible. The last thing we want to hear a surgeon, scalpel in hand, say to us is: "I didn't go to med school, but don't worry. I did read the Bible."

Also, as mentioned earlier, the Bible is made up of many different kinds of literature — poetry for example. Asking if a poem is true is different from asking if a mathematical equation is true. The Psalms of the Bible are poetry. They truly reflect and give voice to the life of faith in all its richness and ambiguity. They are "true" to life. They are *believable*. My point is that not everything in the Bible can be, or should be, believed in the same way. A poem is true even if it is not *literally* true.

There are also places in the Bible in which a literal event takes on symbolic meaning. Jesus healed people. Even his enemies admitted that. Everyone thought that Jesus did amazing and miraculous things. But the "point" of the miracle was not the "Wow!" factor. The miracle was a "sign" which pointed to God and God's kingdom. Through Jesus, God was enforcing the divine claim upon creation thus freeing it from the devil's usurpation.

The writers of the Gospels (Matthew, Mark, Luke, and John) understood this and often recorded both the miracle and the meaning of the miracle. The story of the healing of a man born blind in John 9, is both a story of a physical healing *and* the story of a man coming to see, to believe, in Jesus.

In the same way, Jesus cast out demons. The point of this was to show people that God in Christ had power over evil. Jesus, on occasion, raised the dead. This miracle points us to the truth that God's love is stronger than death. If we miss the meaning of the miracle, we miss the point.

Or again, think about the opening chapters of Genesis. Darwin undermined a literalist reading of the creation stories, but not a theological reading. The essential theological meaning of the first creation story (Genesis 1:1-2:3) is that the Universe was created for a purpose. The purpose was established by God. God is the Author and Goal (*telos*) of Creation. As a matter of fact, I tend to think that the Genesis accounts of creation are not so much about our origins as they are our destination. We're headed towards Paradise, but we keep sinfully derailing God's purposes. We continue to be expelled *east of Eden.*

Also, blind chance or good luck are totally inadequate explanations of the miracle of life. Genesis is God speaking eternal truths revealing where we've come from and where we're going. If you believe that creation has a God-given purpose and a God-given destination, then you believe Genesis. You're a Bible believer and you're using your brain.

Another way the gift of reason helps us to understand the Bible is through critical study. During the 18th and 19th centuries new tools for studying the Bible were developed. These new tools placed the Bible under the microscope of the "historical critical" method.[69] These methods of research raised

---

69. The historical critical method of biblical study is taught in almost all advanced levels of biblical studies. These methods of study include things like redaction criticism, textual criticism, tradition criticism, etc. For a good beginning introduction to these issues see *Biblical Exegesis: A Beginner's Handbook* by John H. Hayes and Carl R. Holladay (Atlanta: John Knox, 1982).

questions about many of the traditional understandings and interpretations of the Bible. Did Moses, as most pre-modern people believed, personally write the first five books of the Bible (the Torah)? Was Paul the author of all the books that bear his name in the New Testament? Was the Earth created in six literal days? All of these questions were answered in the negative.

However, and this is extremely important, none of the new scientific methods of study ever completely disproved the basic historical truths of the Bible. So, for example, when the Old Testament mentions various kings and kingdoms, archeological evidence has largely confirmed the existence of these people and places. The journal *Biblical Archeology Review* (*BAR*) published an article by a Purdue University professor which listed fifty people mentioned in the Old Testament who were confirmed by archeological evidence. So, we're not talking about the kingdom of make believe. The Bible "interprets" history, but it doesn't make it up.

Also, these new methods of studying the Bible caused scholars to search for older and better ancient manuscripts. The science of textual criticism was born. Textual critics began to date, catalogue, and translate these texts. Thousands of ancient manuscripts were collected and studied. Through the work of these scholars we can say with a great deal of confidence that we can know what the ancient authors wrote.

Yes, it is true, for example, that we do not have the original documents of the New Testament. However, the late Bruce Metzger, a renowned New Testament scholar and textual critic, notes:

> We have copies commencing within a couple of generations from the writing of the originals, whereas in the case of other ancient texts, maybe five, eight, or ten centuries elapsed between the original and the earliest surviving copy.[70]

---

70. As quoted by Lee Strobel, *The Case for Christ: A Journalist's Personal Investigation of the Evidence for Jesus* (Grand Rapids: Zondervan, 1998), 76.

The New Testament is undoubtedly the best preserved ancient document in our possession. Frederick Kenyon, who was a Director and Principal Librarian at the British Museum, summed up what we've learned from the science of textual criticism:

> The interval ... between the dates of original composition and the earliest extant evidence becomes so small as to be in fact, negligible, and the last foundation for any doubt that the Scriptures have come down to us substantially as they were written has now been removed. Both the authenticity and the general integrity of the books of the New Testament may be regarded as finally established.[71]

Why go into such detail? Because there is a popular, but terribly mistaken, idea that the New Testament was radically altered by early Christians. It is supposed that it was written long after the events it describes. Worse yet, some suggest that it was written to hide a secret, a great deception. Bestselling novels like *The Da Vinci Code* play into these popular misconceptions. This is intellectual nonsense. Dan Brown, the author of *The Da Vinci Code*, is not an example of a smart, well-read skeptic overcoming the faith of gullible believers. Rather, it's a case of a creative, if ill-informed, writer who can spin a good yarn and make lots of money in the process.

A person may choose for many reasons not to believe the witness of the New Testament. But this choice cannot be based on the erroneous idea of a late and altered New Testament. Here it is straight up: The reasonable truth is that the New Testament is an authentic witness to the faith of the earliest followers of Jesus. They truly believed that Jesus was the risen Lord. If we read the Bible with an open and prayerful mind, we'll reach the same conclusion.

---

71. Frederick Kenyon, *The Bible and Archeology* (New York: Harper, 1940), 288ff.

The Authority of the Bible

The Bible is a historical document written by people of faith for people of faith. It's also a book that has been dissected and scrutinized by the best historical and scientific methods of study available. It's an extraordinary and remarkable collection of ancient writings.

But Christians receive the Bible not just as a work of great historical, literary, and cultural value, but, again, as the *inspired* Word of God in written form. The New Testament scholar Luke Timothy Johnson says it well:

> It is not enough to discover what [the Scriptures] meant in their historical context, as though they were simple human compositions. It is necessary also to be open to their prophetic voice, which can speak to every age and help every age discern the work of the Living God in the present.... The same Holy Spirit that breathes through those texts breathes in human hearts and minds as they read....[72]

The Bible is a "living" Book of the living God. This is what Christians believe. It is what you, as a Christian, or as someone considering becoming a Christian, are asked to believe.

A Lutheran Rule-of-Thumb for Interpreting the Bible: Law and Gospel

> *There is thus a single law, effective in all ages and known to all men because it is written in everyone's heart. From the beginning to the end no one can excuse himself [for] the Spirit never stops speaking this law in the hearts of men.*[73] — Martin Luther

---

72. Luke Timothy Johnson, *The Creed: What Christians Believe and Why It Matters* (New York: Doubleday, 2003), 239.

73. As quoted in *The Theology of Martin Luther*, trans. by Robert C. Schultz (Philadelphia: Fortress Press, 1966), 251-252.

The law is so good and speaks so well of me that it makes my life unbearable to me. — Hans Joachim Iwand

There is also a particularly Lutheran rule-of-thumb to help us understand and interpret the Bible. As noted, Lutheran Christians, like the vast majority of other Christians, read the Bible through the lens of a rule of faith (the creeds), understand Jesus to be the center or God's self-revelation, and make use of the best biblical scholarship. Lutherans also understand and interpret the Bible as God's Word of "law and the gospel." What does this mean?

Martin Luther said that human beings are ultimately "hearers."[74] We hear, or perceive, reality as either friend or foe, for us or against us, gracious or ungracious, life or death, promise or demand. In other words, to use classic Lutheran theological categories, we hear God's Word as *law* or *gospel*. The Bible, as God's word, addresses us as law or gospel, threat and promise, judgment and forgiveness.

Sometimes Christians misunderstand the distinction between law and gospel as the difference between the Old Testament (law) and the New Testament (grace). However, it is *very* important to understand that the gospel can be heard in the Old Testament and the law in the New Testament. There is no simplistic separation between the two testaments.

Traditionally, Lutheran Christians (and some other Protestant Christians) speak of God's law in three distinct, but related and interconnected, ways. These are called the three uses of the law.

The First Use of the Law (the civil use)

Believe it or not, I don't always want to do what's right. Sometimes, I'm tempted to do what I know is wrong. God knows

---

74. Gerhard Ebeling, *Luther: An Introduction to His Thought*, trans. by R.A. Wilson (Philadelphia: Fortress, 1972), 120ff.

that all of us have this problem. So, he graciously gave the law to protect us from each other. The law is like a fence which hinders us from trespassing into a field in which landmines are hidden. If I trespass, bad things happen to me and to those who travel with me. The first use of the law helps me avoid these landmines.

And it's not only me that God is concerned about. He's concerned about my neighbor. There's a fence around my neighbor's house and spouse with a sign that says, "No trespassing! Violators will be subject to the law." God's law protects.

In society, the law functions as a "provisional" means of ordering our life together. No society can flourish without just laws. Laws which seek to protect and secure us from lawbreakers.

The first use of the law is similar to what is known as the natural law. Natural law theory says that there are some truths which are "self-evident." There are some things that "you can't not know." We all know that you shouldn't break into your neighbor's house and steal his stuff. Even the atheist knows this. If you live next door to an atheist, steal his stuff and see if he gets upset.

Much more seriously, at some level everyone knows that child abuse is very, very wrong. This law is implanted in us, "written on our hearts."[75] To try to deny this truth is like trying to deny the law of gravity. Just as there are physical laws written in nature, there are also moral laws written.

Child abuse is evil. This is not a mere cultural taboo. It's a law written in our conscience. If we listen to these kinds of "natural" laws, then we can live reasonably well together. God help us if we don't listen.

To clarify, no one is talking about imposing some Christian form of *sharia law*. The important thing is to recognize that God (or nature if you don't believe in God) speaks to all people of all cultures protective words for the good of all creation.

---

75. Romans 1.

People of goodwill, who disagree on theological issues, believers and unbelievers, can hopefully agree that some things are innately disordered and destructive to humanity's well-being. The theologian Carl Braaten writes:

> Natural law is the enemy of cultural relativism, the notion that laws are mere moral conventions that vary among societies, with no basis in the way things are constituted. That would relegate the ideal of justice to oscillating opinions of human beings. The law of justice must be the same for everyone, so that if murder and rape are morally wrong in America, they are equally so in Asia. Torture is wrong no matter who tries to excuse it. Humans have a God-given right to freedom and equality that should be universally respected and defended.[76]

The law creates a bridge between the Church and society. We can't agree on the doctrine of the Holy Trinity or other specifically Christian beliefs, but we can agree that murder is wrong. You can't not know this! Even an atheist knows this. Only the seriously selfish or the psychopath could try to claim ignorance of this law. The taking of innocent human life is immoral, therefore legal prohibitions are in effect to protect the innocent. This is the reason why historically the Church has condemned abortion. Who is more innocent than an unborn child?

The law which forbids murder is also the basis for laws against medical malpractice, drunk driving, speeding, and many other civil laws. My motivation for keeping the speed limit is not, unfortunately, always because I love my neighbor and am concerned for his or her safety. So where my love falls short, the law steps in. The law restrains sinful drivers like me. It also restrains murderers, thieves, and other misfits by threatening them with punishment.

---

76. Carl E. Braaten, *Essential Lutheranism: Theological Perspectives on Christian Faith and Doctrine* (Delhi, NY: American Lutheran Publicity Bureau, 2012), 178-179.

There's a scene in the movie *O Brother Where Art Thou* in which three escaped prisoners come across a baptismal service taking place in a river. The three convicts stand observing the baptism when suddenly one of them rushes into the water to be baptized. He emerges from the water "saved." Then he tells his two partners: "That's it boys, I been redeemed. The preacher done washed away all my sins and transgressions ... including that Piggly Wiggly I knocked over in Yazoo ... the preacher said that that sin's been washed away too. Neither God nor man's got nothin' on me now." Later, one of his comrades-in-crime, played by George Clooney, responds, "Even if [your baptism] did put you square with the Lord, the state of Mississippi's a little more hard-nosed." The civil use of the law is God's hard-nosed way to "hinder gross transgressions and crimes in this world of sin."

The law is, therefore, God's means to order a more just society. And just societies are dependent upon just citizens. God's law is not a word spoken only to society in general, but to each of us individually. It is "my" gross transgressions which need to be stopped. We often forget that our individual sins are like ripples in a pond caused by a single stone. We *individually* make a positive or negative difference. Often, talk of "social justice" is a cover for our unwillingness to become "personally" just.

The Second Use of the Law (the theological use)

The first use of the law speaks to everyone through the voice of conscience. The biblical law (like the Ten Commandments) amplifies the natural law. We can try to silence it, but never completely. To some extent all of us have a guilty conscience, and for good reason.

The second use of the law is the word God speaks that terrifies us by showing us the beauty of God's holiness, which at the same time reveals the ugliness of our sin. Imagine yourself standing naked before a mirror and comparing yourself to a sculpture or picture of an absolutely perfect human form. You get the point.

70

The law lifts up an ideal from which we have all fallen short. This means more than feeling guilty and being sorry for our sins. The "second use" of the law is also like a finger pointing us to the seeming emptiness, absurdity, futility, and hopelessness of a world devoid of God's presence, love, forgiveness, and grace. Sin, death, and the devil seem to conquer.

God may even seem not to exist, for the law is "a word in which God remains absent and concealed."[77] If he does exist, He's distant and dangerous. The judgment of the law is that life is "nasty, brutish, and short." There is no exit, no justice, and no mercy. The law tells us that everything is ultimately against us. It has no sense of humor. The Universe is very unfriendly indeed.

It's important to understand that when we hear God's word as law, it is not that God wants to torture us with the truth. When we hear God's law, it's like God, the Good Physician, telling the patient how seriously ill he is before prescribing the treatment. After telling us that we have a terminal illness, the Great Physician speaks a word of hope and healing. This is the word of the gospel.

Remember: the gospel of Jesus Christ *is* the center of God's message to us. Jesus is the Word of God made flesh.[78] His life, death, and resurrection — as a singular event in history — is God's most powerful and clear Word assuring us that he is not "against" us, but he is "for" us. God will not abandon humanity to the absurdity of death. God in Jesus will save us from the accusations of the law. God in Christ will forgive us our sins. Our existential well-being is dependent upon which of these words — law or gospel — reaches our inmost being.[79]

I had a seminary professor who told the story of a woman he knew who had many problems. Her problems eventually

---

77. Gerhard Ebeling, *Luther: An Introduction to His Thought*, American Edition (Philadelphia: Fortress Press, 1972), 121.

78. John 1.

79. Ibid., Gerhard Ebeling, 120.

71

caused her to have a complete nervous breakdown. All she could hear was the voice of the law. Everything and everyone seemed to be *against* her.

She entered into a catatonic state and was unresponsive to others. However, her pastor kept visiting her, reading Scripture to her, and praying for her. Each time he visited he spoke into her ear this simple prayer: "Jesus loves you, and he will never let you go." In time, a miraculous thing happened. The woman recovered. Somehow, in the depths of her soul, she heard the gospel and it raised her up.[80]

The Bible is a book filled with law *and* gospel. In other words, it is filled with God's demands *and* promises. These promises offer true hope and comfort to terrified sinners who stand in the presence of God's justice. David Watson, an Anglican priest who died of cancer at an early age, kept a journal of his battle against the disease. In one entry, he describes perfectly the power of the gospel to bring hope and peace:

> As I spent time chewing over the endless assurances and promises to be found in the Bible [the gospel], so my faith in the living God grew stronger and held me safe in his hands. God's word to us, especially his word spoken by the Spirit through the Bible, is the very ingredient that feeds our faith. If we feed our souls regularly on God's word, several times each day, we should become robust spiritually just as we feed on ordinary food several times each day, and become robust physically. Nothing is more important than hearing and obeying the word of God.[81]

Life is hard and each day terrible things happen to people. Each of us is broken. Think of the worst sin you've ever committed. Then, think what it would be like if all you ever heard was a word of accusation. If we only "hear" this word, then we can easily lose our faith, our hope, and our peace.

---

80. With thanks to the Rev. Dr. James A. Nestingen.
81. David Watson, *Fear No Evil: A Personal Struggle with Cancer* (London: Hodder and Stoughton, 1984), 39.

Consider the difference it makes to hear Jesus and his promise of absolute love, forgiveness, and life. This is the word of the gospel which we desperately need to hear. So hear it right now: "For the sake of Jesus Christ, your sins are forgiven. Go, and sin no more."

The Third Use of the Law (ethical guidance for Christians)[82]

Finally, we come to the question of the third use of the law. Simply put, the third use of the law teaches that the law is a guide to faithful living. Christians, and particularly Lutheran Christians, have always had a tendency to flirt with anti-nomianism. This is the idea that since God's grace is so much greater than our sin, and since the gospel assures us of God's forgiveness; therefore we can sin and grace will abound! What is forgotten is what was mentioned earlier: the beauty of God's law.

The law is a beautiful Truth. The life well-lived is a life rightly ordered by God's law. This is why the psalmist of ancient Israel could sing:

> Oh, How I love your law!
> All the day long it is in my mind.
> Your commandment has made me wiser than my enemies,
> And it is always with me....
> I restrain my feet from every evil way,
> That I may keep your word...
> How sweet are your words to my taste![83]

---

82. Historically, there has always been an inter-Lutheran squabble over whether or not the law should be enjoined upon Christians as described here. I won't trouble the reader with the details. Suffice it to say to the Lutherans reading this that whichever side of the debate you may embrace, we all want the same thing. We want Christians to exhibit a certain degree (however imperfectly) of sanctity. In other words, we want the redeemed to look more so.

83. Psalm 119:97-98, 100, 103.

What does it mean to live a good and beautiful life? The law replies: "The life well-lived is a life rightly ordered by God's law." It is a life in which God is both feared and loved, marriage is honored, children are cherished, life is respected, property protected, the sick and suffering are offered care, the hungry food, the homeless shelter. A life directed by God's law bears the marks of grace, dignity, and holiness. Albeit, no life is lived with complete beauty. We always, as Luther noted, remain *simil iustus et peccator*: sinner and saint, ugly and beautiful. Yet, by God's grace, we strive to make something of a beautiful life. God's law is a guide to a life well-lived.

Read It

This chapter began by asking how we can believe that the Bible, which was written all those years ago in a pre-scientific age, can possibly be true. My answer is rather simple: Pick up the Bible and prayerfully read it. As you do so, ask God to speak to you. Don't worry overmuch about evolution and creation or how Noah got all those animals on that ark. These stories are God's Word to us, but God is speaking in perhaps non-literal, but extremely important ways. Read these stories as God's Word trying to break through the stubbornness of the human heart to bring His light and beauty into the darkness and ugliness of this world. Always remember Jesus who is the heart and soul of Scripture. Hear God speaking a Word of law and gospel, demand and promise, judgment and forgiveness, death and life. When you do this, you will discover what I did when I was about 17-years old, and what believers have learned for 2000 years: God is not silent.

Questions for Discussion

1. What is something you find difficult to understand about the Bible?

2. Do you have a favorite Bible passage or story? What is it?

3. Can you think of a story or teaching in the Bible that troubles you?

4. What are the three rules-of-thumb for understanding and interpreting the Bible? What is the other specifically Lutheran rule-of-thumb?

5. What do you think it means to say that the Bible is the Word of God? Can you think of a time when you heard God's Word as law? As gospel?

6. How might the Bible be used to help us understand God's will about difficult moral issues?

7. What are your feelings about religion and politics? Does the Bible have a place in the discussion? Why or why not?

8. What does it mean to you to live a beautiful life?

9. One ancient way of reading the Bible is called *lectio divina*. Simply put, *lectio divina* is the practice of quieting ourselves before God and listening to how the Bible speaks to us in a direct, prayerful, and personal way. Let's look at one passage and open ourselves to hear God's Word as law. Then we'll turn to a passage in which we open ourselves to hear God's word as gospel.

   Law: Matthew 25:41-46

   Gospel: Matthew 11:28-30

Have one member of your group read it out loud. Now, each read it silently. Prayerfully ask God to speak to your heart and mind. What is Christ calling us to do? What does it mean to take his yoke upon us? How can we learn from Jesus? What is God saying to you?

Chapter 4
Why Did God Become Man?
The Word Incarnate

Why aren't we all on the most wanted list?
— Robert W. Jenson

God goes to every man when sore bestead,
Feeds body and spirit with his bread;
For Christians, pagans alike he hangs dead,
And both alike forgiving. — Dietrich Bonhoeffer
Letters and Papers from Prison

The cross alone is our theology. — Martin Luther

We all know that there is something terribly wrong with this world. Things are not the way they're supposed to be. *We* are not the way *we're* supposed to be. What's wrong with us? Why can't we just get along?

According to the Christian faith, the problem which needs fixing is sin. Sin is all that separates us from God. Alienated from God, we are thereby also estranged from each other, and even within our own selves. I can't figure myself out. I can say, think, or do things about which I'm ashamed. "Is it not the case," writes Benedict XVI, "that our need to be reconciled with God — the silent, mysterious, seemingly absent, and yet omnipresent God — is the real problem of the whole of world history?"[84] This is the problem that humanity, no how matter hard we try, cannot solve.

---

84. Benedict XVI, *Jesus of Nazareth: Part II* (San Francisco: Ignatius Press, 2011), 79.

Perhaps no modern writer could depict the reality of humanity's alienation from God more powerfully than the late Flannery O'Connor. In one of her short stories, "A Good Man is Hard to Find," she tells a disturbing tale of a family riding through the southern countryside on a beautiful summer day. Unfortunately, things turn very ugly when they randomly meet and are accosted by a band of escaped convicts. The dark tale unfolds as the convicts decide to kill the family, take the car, and run. Each of the family is led away to their doom. We are spared the gruesome details. However, the leader of this band of thugs, who is known simply as the "Misfit," has a conversation with the elderly Grandmother just before she is murdered. The Misfit says:

> "Jesus was the only One that ever raised the dead, and He shouldn't have done it. He thrown everything off balance. If He did what He said, then it's nothing for you to do but throw away everything and follow Him, and if He didn't, then it's nothing for you to do but enjoy the few minutes you got left the best way you can — by killing somebody or burning down his house or doing some other meanness to him. No pleasure but meanness," he said and his voice had become almost a snarl.

> "Maybe He didn't raise the dead," the old lady mumbled, not knowing what she was saying and feeling so dizzy that she sank down in the ditch with her legs twisted under her.

> "I wasn't there so I can't say He didn't," the Misfit said. "I wisht I had of been there," he said, hitting the ground with his fist. "It ain't right I wasn't there because if I had of been there I would of known. Listen lady," he said in a high voice, "if I had of been there I would of known and I wouldn't be like I am now.[85]

If you don't know that story, let me assure you, it doesn't end well. The Misfit represents humanity alienated from God. If

---

85. Flannery O'Connor, "A Good Man is Hard to Find," *The Complete Stories* (New York: Farrar, Straus and Giroux, 1971), 132.

we continue in our alienation, there won't be a happy ending for us either.

While fortunately most of us manage not to murder each other (at least not literally), we still all share the Misfit's fundamental, fallen, distorted, alienated nature. This is what the Church calls *original sin*. This is the underlying problem of human existence. We are conceived and born into a world alienated from God, our neighbor, and ourselves. Soon we turn on one another and life becomes an endless cycle of meanness. This meanness is evident in bullying, backbiting, betrayals, and every act of barbarism known to us. We've grown accustomed to this unfortunate reality, but it's *not* supposed to be like this.

Still, God is at work. Grace, you will remember, is God at work. God is at work and God loves all people, even Misfits, and desires to save and befriend the lot of us. But how does God begin to make things right? How are Misfits made Fit? What is God doing to break the cycle of meanness? God gives God's life for us — enter the cross.

The cross of Christ is what God does to solve our *real* problem.

The Cross of Christ

Walk into any Christian church of almost any denomination and you will undoubtedly notice one similarity. There is a cross in the front of the church. The cross may be plain or it may depict the image of the crucified or risen Christ. The cross is not accidental or incidental. As we saw in chapter one, the cross conveys a deep theological message about the God in whom Christians believe — the Crucified God. God was truly "in" Christ reconciling the world to himself.[86] In other words, the cross is God's way of healing the breach between himself and humanity.

---

86. II Corinthians 5:19.

A word of caution to the curious reader. Here we need to dig deep. To plumb the depths of the cross is no easy thing. Brilliant minds have done so and each has offered differing opinions and insights. My goal is to help the reader gain a glimpse of just how deep, disturbing, and wondrous the cross is.

The Difference One Little "iota" Makes

What follows concerns a theological fine point which some might think a little too fine. Is this another case of the proverbial ivory tower thinking divorced from "the *real* world"? Here, I ask for the reader's forbearance. We must delve into some deeper waters. It has everything to do with what is real.

One of the greatest theological controversies in the Church took place in the 4th century. It concerned the question: "Who is Jesus and what is his relationship to God?" In many ways, this is the question the Gospels were written to answer. However, the Church continued to struggle with it long after the Gospels were written.

In brief, the issue centered on whether or not, when we meet Jesus, we meet "true God" or simply a representative of God who was closely allied to God, but not "true God." In other words, is God fully and truly present in the humanity of Jesus? Is Jesus mysteriously, but truly, God and Man?

Rivers of theological ink were spilled over this controversy. The controversy came to a head over two Greek words. Some said that the human Jesus shared God's true nature (in Greek *homoousios*). Others insisted that Jesus was a representative of God who shared in a nature "like" God's, but was not fully divine (in Greek *homoiousios* — note that the spelling differs by only one iota).

Why is this theological hair splitting so important? Because when we look at the cross of Christ, we must ask whether we *really* see the "crucified God" or a third party detached from God. Is God looking down from heaven wringing his hands in anguish over what's happening to Jesus? Or, is God looking out from the cross at the world which is murdering Him? The importance of this question is highlighted by the theologian Miroslav Volf:

> By "putting forward" the Son, as the apostle Paul wrote, isn't the Father abusing the Son? Doesn't substitution constitute wrong doing, this time against the innocent Christ...? The Father would be abusing the Son and committing a divine wrongdoing ... if Christ were a third party, [apart from] God who was wronged and humanity who wronged God. But he isn't. He stands firmly on the side of the forgiving God, not between the forgiving God and forgiven humanity....What happened when God "made him [Christ] to be sin who knew no sin, so that in him we might become the righteousness of God" (2 Corinthians 5:21)? The answer is simple: God placed human sin on God...! The God who is One beyond numbering and yet mysteriously Three reconciled us by shouldering our sin in the person of Christ who is one of the Three.... The One who was offended bears the burden of the offence.[87]

Note those words, "God placed human sin on God." Christianity teaches that God united himself with Jesus' humanity in such a way that God truly experienced the brunt of human sin, suffering, and death. This is not some "ivory tower" theological speculation. The cross of Christ reveals the God who loves us enough to suffer and die in order to save us. God, in other words, truly feels our pain.

Some theologians and Christian mystics have even speculated that God Himself was *somehow* altered by the sufferings endured in His Incarnation. That is, when God became a human being in the human nature of Jesus. In the Nicene Creed we confess our catholic faith in Jesus Christ who is: "true God from true God, begotten, not made, of one Being (*homoousios*)

---

87. Miroslav Volf, *Free of Charge*, 144-145.

with the Father." Christianity teaches that the "true God" entered into human history through the humanity of Jesus *in order to reconcile humanity to Himself.* That is, to heal our separation and alienation from God and begin to make the world like it's supposed to be and we like we're supposed to be.

Understanding the Atonement

So, what was God *in* Jesus doing on the cross? Why was it necessary? The Bible says that Jesus — the God/Man — was atoning for the sins of humanity *in order to save us.* Jesus' death on the cross was a "sacrifice of atonement."[88] If we take the word atonement apart, we immediately see its definition: At-One-Ment. The Atonement is about what God did for us through the cross of Christ in order to bridge the chasm between humanity and God. Traditionally, the Atonement has most often been understood by Christians in three complementary ways:

1. Reconciliation

As we saw at the beginning of this chapter, our alienation from God is our greatest problem. God's goal in coming to us in Christ was to reconcile us to Himself. Two passages from the Bible are particularly germane:

> So if anyone is in Christ, there is a new creation: everything old has passed away; see, everything has become new! All this is from God who reconciled us to himself through Christ, and has given us the ministry of reconciliation; that is, in Christ God was reconciling the world to himself, not counting their trespasses against them and entrusting the message of reconciliation to us. So we are ambassadors for Christ, since God is making his appeal through us; we entreat you on behalf of Christ, be reconciled to God. For our sake he made him to be

88. Romans 3:25.

sin who knew no sin, so that in him we might become the righteousness of God.[89]

For if while we were enemies we were reconciled to God through the death of his Son, much more surely, having been reconciled, will we be saved by his life."[90]

On the cross God in Christ is seeking to break through the hardened and sinful hearts of Misfits in order to reveal His goodness and grace. Gerhard Forde explains: "God cannot and does not need to be bought, even by Jesus, before God can be forgiving. God out of love and mercy sends Jesus to forgive. God's problem is how to get through to us, how to get through to people who aspire to be gods, and who are thus bent on getting rid of God."[91]

On the cross Jesus, the God Man, was murdered. *We —* the collective human race — are guilty of deicide. Why would we murder God? Because there's no room in this world for the god I want to be and the God who is. We sinners resist reconciliation because if we discover that God is real and wants us to reconcile our lives to the divine life, then suddenly we can't be "like we are now." God forbid, I might have to (*gulp*) admit that I'm wrong. I might need to repent. Misfits don't always appreciate being made fit. It's a lot easier and less painful to get rid of this God who disturbs us.

"The grace of God," writes Cornelius Plantinga, "always comes to us with blood on it. What had we thought the ripping and writhing of Golgotha were all about?"[92] The cross of Christ is God "ripping and writhing" His way to us through the flesh of Jesus in order to awaken us to His love and reconcile us to Himself. From the cross God is saying to us, "This is

---

89. II Corinthians 5:17-21.

90. Romans 5:10, cf. also Colossians 1:20ff.

91. Gerhard Forde, *Theology is for Proclamation* (Minneapolis: Fortress Press, 1990), 124.

92. Cornelius Plantinga, Jr., *Not the Way It's Supposed to Be: A Breviary of Sin* (Grand Rapids: Eerdmans, 1995), 199.

how much I love you and want to be your Friend. Be reconciled to me!"

2. Satisfaction/Substitution

The Atonement is perhaps most often understood as the means by which Jesus substituted himself for all humanity. *Somehow* (and the devil is indeed in the details), our sins were "transferred" to Jesus. Jesus "bore our sins in his body on the cross,"[93] and made "peace through his blood, shed on the cross."[94] Jesus' death on the cross is understood as the perfect, holy sacrifice offered to God for the sins of the world. Picture yourself in a courtroom standing before the Judge. God is the Judge, and you are found to be *guilty as sin*, and sentenced to die.

Modern people often have trouble with this idea. We tend to think most people are "basically good." But what if the opposite is true? What if underneath the veneer of respectability we're all misfits?

When I was about 20 years old, I had an experience when praying. Prayer was relatively new to me. I was in an apartment kneeling. Suddenly, I had sort of an inner vision. In my mind's eye, I saw me striking Jesus on the face. Like an epiphany I realized that in each of my own immature and sinful actions I had slapped Jesus. I crucified him. At that point, I began to understand what it meant to be a sinner. I was not "basically good." I was a misfit. To be sure, in the hall of Misfits I was in the minors, but still, I wasn't nearly as good as I'd imagined. On the cross of Christ, "we see the rendering of the verdict on the gravity of sin.... None of our sins are small or of little account."[95] Every *supposedly* small act of selfishness, greed, lust, gluttony, sloth, and pride is an act that kills the life of God. We all have the Blood of God on our hands.

---

93. I Peter 2:24.

94. Colossians 1:20.

95. Richard John Neuhaus, *Death on a Friday Afternoon: Meditations on the Last Words of Jesus on the Cross* (New York: Basic Books, 2000), 18-19.

84

It is not my desire here to make anyone feel more guilty or ashamed than we probably already do. My desire is to correct a distorted image of God and ourselves. Simply put, our awareness of sin has slipped. "Nowadays," Cornelius Plantinga, Jr. writes, "the accusation *you have sinned* is often said with a grin, and with a tone that signals an inside joke. At one time, this accusation still had the power to jolt people."[96] Stop a minute and think about it: You have offended God. Let that sink into your mind.

Sin is not a trivial slight against a distant deity. It's an offense against the absolute holiness of a very present God. Let's turn the tables. Think of a time when you personally were sinned against. The slightest offence can wound us. Friendships are sundered because of a social snub. We remember and review the sins others have committed, and relish the idea of revenge. There is an innate sense of wanting justice. So when we read of someone breaking into a home, tying up the husband, raping his wife and daughter, and then setting the house on fire, we instinctively cry for justice — or vengeance. There are vestiges of righteous anger even in the unrighteous.

If we who are unrighteous are still able to understand evil and long for the punishment of evildoers; how much more is God's pure righteousness offended by sin? To understand the cross of Christ we must recognize the depth of the offence against God. Justice must be served. "It is a fearful thing to fall into the hands of the living God."[97] And yet, God loves us. This is the divine predicament.

So on the cross God's justice and God's love meet. "Righteousness and peace" kiss each other."[98] Miroslav Volf says it eloquently:

God doesn't forgive until the demands of justice have been satisfied.... How is God's justice "satisfied"? How

---

96. Ibid, Cornelius Plantinga, Jr., *Not the Way it's Supposed to Be*, ix.

97. Hebrews 10:31.

98. Psalm 85:10.

is the forgiveness of sins "purchased"? That satisfaction, that purchase, occurred when Jesus Christ took our place, insisted Luther: "Christ, the Son of God, stands in our place and has taken all our sins on his shoulders.... He is the eternal satisfaction for our sins and reconciles us with God, the Father." God forgives because Christ paid what we owed.... Christ was condemned in our place.[99]

Note what is said here: "God forgives because Christ paid what we owed." The scales of divine justice written into the fabric of the cosmos must be satisfied. The Universe is not only ultimately warm and loving, it is a place in which justice is supposed to dwell. How could it be otherwise if God is truly good? Would we want God to "wink" at the Holocaust? Were the people responsible for such heinous atrocities "basically good"? On the cross, the divine love in Christ Jesus died to satisfy divine justice.

3. Redemption

A third illustration of the Atonement is seen when we move from the courtroom to the marketplace.

Young people who were confirmed in the Lutheran Church may (or at least should) remember a passage from *The Small Catechism* which often has to be memorized. It is the explanation to the Second Article of the Apostles' Creed. This second article rehashes the basics of the life, death, and resurrection of Jesus. The explanation in part says:

I believe that Jesus Christ, true God, Son of the Father from all eternity, and also true Man born of the Virgin Mary, is my Lord. At great cost he has saved and redeemed me, not with silver and gold, *but with his holy and precious blood and his innocent sufferings and death* (emphasis added).

On the cross, Jesus Christ died to redeem us from sin, death, and the devil. His "holy and precious" blood was given as the

99. Miroslav Volf, *Free of Charge*, 144-145.

price of our redemption. We were, says St. Paul, "bought with a price."[100] And again, "Christ redeemed us from the curse of the law by becoming a curse for us."[101] Jesus defined His mission on earth as, "not to be served, but to serve, and to give his life as a ransom for many."[102]

The New Testament depicts Jesus' death as a means by which God ransomed the world from its bondage to sin and death. In the ancient world, a "ransom" was almost a "technical term ... for the purchase of manumission of a slave."[103] On the cross, Jesus paid the price, the ransom, to free us from sin and death. Of course, the logical question is, "To whom did He pay the ransom?"

Some early Christians wondered if the life of Christ was sacrificed as a payment to the devil. Through our Fall into the condition of sin, the devil had ensnared humanity in the trap of sin and death. The devil, the "god of this world,"[104] was offered the life of Christ as a ransom for humanity. The devil accepted the ransom, but was outwitted when God raised the ransom from the dead.

Others repudiated this idea thinking that it gave the devil too much authority and power. They insisted, as mentioned above, that God paid the ransom to Himself to satisfy divine justice. Now, rather than living in slavish fear, guilt, and shame; we are set free. The price for our manumission is paid. We are redeemed, and it cost God His life.

Perhaps most importantly, Christ's death as a ransom is descriptive of how many Christians "experience" faith. When Misfits come to Christ (and when Christ comes to them), they often say things like: "I was enslaved to money, or sex, or drugs,

---

100. I Corinthians 6:18-20, cf. 7:23.

101. Galatians 3:13.

102. Mark 10:45.

103. John Stott, *The Cross of Christ*, 176.

104. II Corinthians 4:4.

or alcohol, or work, or success, or fame, or anger, or gambling, or guilt, etc. Christ redeemed me from this." Christ sets us free.

However, sometimes well-meaning Christians make the Christian life sound like a walk in the park. Freedom is painted in such clear terms as to make it sound that there is no more struggle. We hear glowing testimonies of people who are immediately set free from sin. Sainthood is bestowed freely and without any required sanctification. "It's easy," they say, "all you have to do is believe in Jesus." Which brings us to the last point.

Justification by Grace through Faith ("What must I do to be saved?")[105]

In whatever ways we prefer to illustrate the Atonement (reconciliation, satisfaction, or redemption), the heart of the matter is that on the cross, God is seeking to heal the breach which separates us from him. God bears the burden, pays the price, and satisfies the need for justice written into the fabric of the cosmos.

When we hear this message (the gospel), and entrust ourselves to its promises, we are saved, or justified. This is what justification by faith means.[106] Martin Luther wrote that this doctrine reveals "the true meaning of Christianity."[107] Why is justification by faith so important?

---

105. It should be noted here that after nearly 500 years of distrust and disagreement, in October of 1999, the Lutheran World Federation and the Vatican signed *The Joint Declaration on the Doctrine of Justification*. The mutual condemnations over this doctrine were withdrawn and considered no longer applicable to the Lutheran churches who signed this declaration or to the contemporary Roman Catholic Church.

106. Romans 5:1, Galatians 2:15ff.

107. *Luther's Works, Lectures on Galatians* (1535, Vol. 26) eds. Jaroslav Pelikan and Walter A. Hansen (St. Louis: Concordia Publishing House), 136. Also see *The Cross of Christ*, John Stott, 182. Within Lutheranism, justification by faith came to be understood as the doctrine by which the Church stands or falls (*articulus stantis et cadentis ecclesiae*). Cf. WA 40/3.352.3.

One theologian said that the doctrine of justification by faith is the Church's "crap detector."[108] What kind of "crap" does it detect? It detects the foul odor of both unrighteousness and self-righteousness. How so?

First, when a person believes the gospel of Jesus Christ, he or she begins to realize that sin stinks. Before Christ, we're like those unfortunates who, to put it bluntly, can't smell themselves. But once we've gotten a whiff of Jesus, once we've smelled the odor of the gospel of grace; then we begin to notice the difference between a rose and a cesspool. This happens when we get a scent of the "fragrance of the knowledge" of Christ Jesus.[109] Conversion happens when we finally admit it, "I need a bath."

Second, justification by faith detects the odor of self-righteousness. The self-righteous are those who admit that everyone *else* stinks. They don't deny that sin is rank, but it's always someone else's sin that reeks. They have faith, but it's faith in their own cleanliness. They cringe at the thought of being associated with the great unwashed. The goal is to remain squeaky clean.

To make matters worse, the self-deluded self-righteous (just in case) seek to cover the smell with the deodorant of respectability and religion. It is a cover up. Have you ever smelled the sickening sweet aroma of those who try too hard to cover a foul stench? But the gospel offers hope for the self-righteous too. Once the self-righteous get a whiff of Jesus, they also confess: "I need a bath."

Faith is taking the much-needed bath. Unbelief is refusing the bath. What about you? Need a bath? The promise of the gospel, verified by the experience of myriads of Christians, is that "the blood of Jesus Christ cleanses us from all sin."[110] We're washed in both blood and water.[111] Baptism is the bath to which we are all called to take.

---

108. Attributed to the Rev. Dr. Gerhard Forde.

109. II Corinthians 2:14.

110. I John 1:7.

111. John 19:34.

Conclusion

I began this chapter with the story of a Misfit. His life was a mess. It stank. So God comes into the mess of this world filled with the stench of death and disease. He comes in Jesus not to judge or condemn us. He comes to cleanse us. In order to present us to the Father, washed, redeemed, reconciled, and forgiven. So that we might become "the aroma of Christ to God."[112]

Questions for Discussion

1. Look at today's newspaper. What stinks to high heaven?

2. What stories are a fragrant aroma pleasing to God?

3. Have you ever been asked if you were saved? If so, how did you respond?

4. Think about and discuss the three pictures of the Atonement presented: Reconciliation, Satisfaction, and Redemption. Which of these illustrations speaks to you most personally?

5. How is the doctrine of justification by faith a "crap detector"?

6. Which is worse, self-righteousness or unrighteousness? Why?

7. It is common for many Christians to "make the sign of the cross" (genuflect). What gave rise to this tradition? Do you feel that this is a meaningful tradition? Why or why not?

8. Many people wonder about the salvation of non-Christians. Is it possible to be saved "apart from" what God has done for us on the cross? Most traditional Christians respond by saying something like: "We cannot be saved apart from Christ, but many may be saved through Christ who did not know him in this life." In other words, we can be saved apart from the Church, but not apart from Jesus. Do you agree? Disagree?

---

112. II Corinthians 2:15.

Chapter 5
What Does God Want Us to Do?
The Call of God

Tonight a mother is singing her child a lullaby. A nurse in a clinic without electricity is holding the hand of a man dying from AIDS. A hungry boy is sharing a scrap of food with his sister. They are not kings — now. But the gospel turns our assumptions about what is lasting, what is significant, what is 'elite' upside down. — Andy Crouch

Love God and do as you please. — St. Augustine

Think nothing and do nothing without a purpose directed to God. For to journey without direction is wasted effort. — St. Mark the Ascetic (5th century)

Each of us is willed, each of us is loved, each of us is necessary. — Pope Benedict XVI

I know a guy who went to law school, but never practiced law. He spent three years of his life learning what he didn't want to do. That's three years well spent. He could have spent thirty years learning the same lesson.

Today, he runs a music store which caters to those who love acoustic guitars, mandolins, banjos and other stringed instruments. It's a great place, and he's doing what he feels *called* to do. Help people make music. That's an admirable calling.

What about you, are you doing what you feel called to do? Let's face it. Many people are unhappy and unsatisfied with their jobs. When I was a freshman in college I read

The Secret Lives of Walter Mitty. Some people found it funny. I found it frightening. Walter was a henpecked husband who never had the courage to follow his heart, so he lived in his head, in a world of daydreams. He never fulfilled a dream.

In the last chapter, we learned that Christians believe that through the cross of Christ, God justifies us and reconciles us to Himself. Reconciled to God, we are now ready to be used to fulfill God's purposes in the world. In other words, we are saved by faith, but saved for what? What do we do with our lives once God gives them back to us?

The Purpose-Given Life

One of the most successful Christian publishing stories of recent times is the phenomenal popularity of Rick Warren's *The Purpose Driven Life.* It is a book that has been used in thousands of congregations across denominational lines. The spinoffs from the original books include *40 Days of Purpose, The Purpose Driven Church, The Purpose Driven Life Journal,* etc. Why is this book such a huge publishing success?

The answer is that Pastor Rick Warren, in plain language with many anecdotes and illustrations, tells people that their lives are *not* meaningless or insignificant. God has a purpose for each of us. And, now get this. We can live that purpose every day no matter who we are or what we do. Knowing our God-given purpose fills our lives with meaning. It full-fills us *because* human beings are created by God in order to further God's purposes on earth. God's purposes "fit" humanity like hand to glove. God calls each of us to be the glove for His Hand. This is our *vocation* or calling.

No Little People

Everyone, no matter how seemingly small or insignificant, is endowed with grandeur.

Each human being bears the image of God. "If there is a God of infinite love and goodness of whom every person is an image," writes philosopher David Bentley Hart, "then certain moral conclusions must be drawn...."[113] These "moral conclusions" include the right of every human being, no matter how poor, disabled, diseased, or reprobate to enjoy the "absolute law of charity."[114]

This sounds great. But is this true? Aren't there a lot of unnecessary people in this world? And, aren't there circumstances when a particular human being, like the seriously disabled, might be excluded?

For example, what happens when prenatal genetic tests indicate that an unborn child will suffer from some disease like cystic fibrosis or developmental delay like Down Syndrome? Many people would argue that "compassion" in such cases allows for a termination of pregnancy. How could such a "defective" person further God's purposes?

Other factors in the decision to terminate the pregnancy include the emotional and economic burden upon the family and society. This child is going to be expensive. Insurance companies may even pressure a family to abort the unborn. In situations like this, abortions are increasingly — and disturbingly — routine. But should these innocents pay such a price for our lack of compassion? Every expectant parent wants the perfect child, but by what standards do we measure perfection? Might God have a purpose for even the most seriously disabled person?

I have a young woman in our congregation who suffers from severe mental retardation. We'll call her Tammy. Tammy's father and mother have spent the last 30 years caring for her. They have made many personal sacrifices in order to give their daughter the best care available. This, undoubtedly, has been more difficult than most of us can ever know. Nevertheless, Tammy's parents have borne this difficulty with grace, patience, love, joy, and faith.

---

113. David Bentley Hart, *Atheist Delusions*, 238.

114. Ibid., 214

Recently I stopped by their home to give Tammy communion. She is blind, and her speech is limited. One word that she often uses is "bela." She sometimes says "bela" after the prayers. "Bela" is her "amen.

As I sat with Tammy and her mother around the table preparing the wine and bread for communion, it suddenly occurred to me that I was in the presence of something very, very holy. It was one of the "holiest" communions I've ever experienced. I was in the presence of Christ — not only Christ in the bread and wine — but Christ in Tammy and her mother. For anyone to suggest that because of her disabilities she does not have a place at the Table of Christ would be — and I choose my words carefully here — demonic.

There is something extremely misguided, even malevolent, when people begin to assume that a purposeful and meaningful life can only be lived by the healthy, the beautiful, the wealthy, and those with higher IQs. The Christian faith asserts that God has a purpose for this world, and that *every* human being is called to play a role in fulfilling God's purposes. For some members of the human race, their calling may be simply to be recipients of love, care, and compassion.

God's Plans and God's Purposes

Before we think more specifically about what God wants us specifically to do, it's necessary to distinguish between a "plan" and a "purpose." Does God have an unalterable plan for each of the seven billion human beings on this Earth? A plan which is specifically for you which God conceived from the beginning of the universe? *If* this is true, then clearly all of us messed up that plan fairly early in life. Rather, it was messed up even before we were born. What if, according to God's plan, my parents weren't supposed to be married to each other? Or my grandparents? The truth is that God's plan was foiled when Adam and Eve fell from grace. We fallen human beings routinely "mess up" God's plans. However, God's purposes never change. When we know that we've "messed up," then the best course of action is to realign our lives with the "divine intentionality." The Christian life is always about connecting and reconnecting our lives to God's purposes.[115]

This does *not* mean that God is uninterested in our plans. God is present to guide us in all of our decisions. When we make important decisions, we should pray for God's guidance and seek wise counsel from people who are attuned to God's voice. However, we should avoid the idea that God's plan for each of us is written on an eternal stone in heaven outlining our lives from birth to death.

Ideally, our lives are lived with both a commitment to fulfill God's purposes and a God-inspired plan outlining how we can accomplish these purposes. Wisdom is knowing our purpose and forming a plan. Unfortunately, we often err when we make plans and forget our purpose, or we have a purpose and fail to plan.

To give just one example, I have had many couples come to the church seeking to be married. The amount of time and money that go into wedding "plans" is often enormous. The couple plans for the ceremony, the reception, the dinner, the menu, the wedding dress, the tuxedos, the colors, who to invite, the limo, the flowers, the seating arrangements, the wedding party, the choice of best man and maid or matron of honor, the flower girl, the ring bearer, the bridesmaids, the ushers, the music, and of course, the honeymoon. Inevitably all the planning leads to emotional and often financial stress. While all the plans are being made, the engaged couple sometimes forgets the "purpose" of the wedding. The purpose of the wedding is the marriage. The wedding "ceremony" is the seal of a lifelong union in which a man and a woman commit their lives to a God-given purpose. Their purpose as husband and wife is living together to serve God, each other, their neighbor, and the children that God may give them. It is an accident waiting

---

115. Robert Benne, *Ordinary Saints: An Introduction to the Christian Life* (Minneapolis: Fortress Press, 2003), 102-103.

to happen if a couple embarks on something as important as marriage and the planning takes precedence over the purpose. Simply put, there is no correlation between success in marriage and the amount of time and money spent on the wedding.

Equally foolish is to have a purpose without a plan. Weddings do need to be planned. Any worthwhile purpose needs a plan in order to accomplish it. Michelangelo had a "plan" in mind before he ever put hammer and chisel to marble when creating his magnificent *David*.

Consider a young person who decides that she wants to go into medicine. She has a purpose that is consistent with God's purposes. God wants to bring healing into the world, and God regularly uses people endowed with medical knowledge to accomplish this. To want to help the sick and suffering, and to be part of the healing process, is a good God-given purpose. However, having a purpose without a plan is simply to squander our life. If this young woman wants to be a physician and help bring healing to the world, then she must plan to study, to work, to prepare herself for the purposes she believes God wants to accomplish through her. God gives us our purpose, and God helps us to plan to fulfill that purpose.

What Does God Want Me to Do?

In Monty Python's religious spoof *The Life of Brian,* Jesus is heard preaching the famous beatitudes. Unfortunately, someone misunderstands him. When Jesus says, "Blessed are the peacemakers," a person thinks that Jesus is saying, "Blessed are the cheese makers." Those who hear this are dumbfounded. Whatever could this mean? "Obviously," says one of the characters, "it isn't to be taken literally. It refers to any manufacturer of dairy products."

The humor makes a serious point. People can misunderstand what God is saying, and do foolish, and sometimes, terrible, things. Near where I grew up there was a large church that taught the members that it was wrong to seek medical care.

96

God would heal and seeking the aid of physicians was evidence of a "lack of faith." People died. Innocent children died.

How do we avoid mishearing God? One way is to learn from mistakes like the one mentioned above. We can also learn from Church history. Historically, God's call, has tended to be misheard in two opposite ways: a Roman Catholic distortion and a Protestant distortion.[116]

The Roman Catholic Distortion

In traditional Roman Catholicism, there is a "higher" calling and a "lower" calling. The higher calling of God refers primarily to the calling into "religious" life as a priest, nun, monk, etc. "Vocations" are primarily understood as "religious." The Church Father, Eusebius, a man who wrote the first history of the Church in the early 4th century, spoke of the "perfect life" by which he meant the celibate and contemplative life, and the "permitted life" by which he meant work and family. James Martin, a Jesuit priest, tells the story of participating in a religious education class as a child. The children were given a small drawing to color. On the top of the page was written Vocations. The left side of the page depicted a married couple with children. Underneath the picture it said "Good." On the right side of the page was a picture of a priest and a nun. Beneath that picture was the word "Better."[117] Father Martin says that this was a "holdover of an older theology," but it is definitely a theology still alive and well in some contemporary Roman Catholic thought.[118]

---

116. Os Guinness, *The Call: Finding and Fulfilling the Central Purpose of Your Life* (Nashville: W Publishing Group, a Division of Thomas Nelson), 31ff.

117. James Martin, *The Jesuit Guide to (Almost) Everything: A Spirituality for Real Life* (New York: HarperOne, 2010), 340-341.

118. For a defense of the traditional, and I believe theologically distorted, view of the superiority of celibacy, see Patricia Snow's article, "Dismantling the Cross" (*First Things*, April, 2015), 33-42.

This traditional two tier concept of calling contributed in many ways to various scandals and abuses within the Church. The clergy came to be seen as those who, because they were closer to God, controlled God's grace. The Church increasingly became "rigidly hierarchical, and spiritually aristocratic."[119] Many Christians criticized this, but it took a certain Augustinian monk named Martin Luther to spark a revolt. He began to question the system. In *The Babylonian Captivity of the Church*, he wrote:

> The works of monks and priests, however holy and arduous they be, do not differ one whit in the sight of God from the works of the rustic laborer in the field or the woman going about her household tasks, but that all works are measured before God by faith alone.... Indeed, the menial housework of a manservant or maidservant is often more acceptable to God than all the fastings and other work of monk or priest, because the monk or priest lacks faith.[120]

Luther was attacking a system which led people to believe that their lives were less pleasing to God if they chose marriage, family, and lay vocations rather than vocations within the hierarchy of the Church. Luther wanted each person to know that God calls us to seek faithfully to fulfill God's purposes in every station of life. If you are a teacher, then you are called by God to be a teacher who glorifies God. This doesn't mean that each morning you write "Jesus loves you" on the classroom board, but it does mean that you seek to impart knowledge, wisdom, and moral integrity to those whom God has put under your charge. If you are an auto mechanic it means that you do your job to the best of your ability, not cheating your customers, but working honestly, diligently, and intelligently. Parents are called by God to raise their children faithfully (a job that definitely

---

119. Guinness 33.

120. *Luther's Works*, American Edition, 55 vols. Eds. Pelikan and Lehmann (St. Louis & Philadelphia: Concordia & Fortress, 1955), 36:78.

requires divine assistance!). In every vocation of life, God calls us to fulfill his purposes faithfully and creatively.

So what is God calling you to do? Probably nothing too glamourous. It's in the mundane that we find our God-given purpose. Helping our neighbor, loving our families, supporting our churches, serving the needs of others, the list goes on and on.

The Protestant Distortion

Protestants sought to correct the Catholic distortion. However, this attempt was all-too-soon distorted in another direction. After the Protestant Reformation, the western world went through the historical process known as the Enlightenment. This was a period of intense scientific and technological progress. It was also a time of great questioning. Loosened from the authority of the Church, scholars began to explore and question the past certainties of faith. When the existence of the biblical God was seriously questioned, so was the idea of God's calling. Without a Caller, there was no sense of call. "Slowly such words as *work, trade, employment,* and *occupation* came to be used interchangeable with *calling* or *vocation.*"[121] In very many ways we still live with this "Protestant Distortion."

A pastor I know had a member of the congregation who was a wealthy businessman. He owned a factory, and one day invited the pastor to come for a tour of the business. It was impressive. The man had built a small empire employing nearly 100 people. Business was booming. As they walked through the factory and conversed, the pastor asked, "How does your Christian faith influence how you run your business?" The man stopped, looked directly into the eyes of his pastor and said, "The two have absolutely nothing to do with each other."

121. Ibid., Guinness, 39.

This is a perfect example of the Protestant distortion. What we do on Sunday morning often has little to do with what we do on Monday morning. God's call may be heard in relation to our "religious" lives, but we remain deaf to the call of God over "every" area of our lives.

Our contemporary, *enlightened* world is one which swims in an ocean of unbelief. While America is certainly a very religious culture — even a confusedly Christian culture — the pervading influences of secularism and skepticism cast shadows of doubt on almost all religious faith and teaching. To quote the atheist Sam Harris: "The only demons we must fear are those that lurk inside every human mind: ignorance, hatred, greed, and *faith*."[122] When faith becomes a demon which must be exorcized, then living life under the call of God becomes (at best) an exercise in foolishness. Christians must ask themselves: Do I have a "job" or a "vocation"? Is my life more about fulfilling God's purposes or paying the bills?

Correcting the Distortions

Fortunately, today both Protestants and Catholics are trying to correct these distortions. For example, Charles Chaput, the Roman Catholic Archbishop of Philadelphia sounds much like Luther:

> When we use the word 'vocation' in Catholic circles, we often think of a call to the priesthood or religious life, but in fact it means much more. 'Vocation' involves keeping house, raising kids, banging out letters on a word processor, hauling garbage, teaching school, selling shoes, practicing law, covering city hall, and making loans. Vocation can be the length and breadth of any life lived for God. The faith and Christian commitment we bring to our work make it our vocation.[123]

---

122. Harris, *The End of Faith*, 226.

123. Charles J. Chaput, *Living the Catholic Faith: Rediscovering the Basics* (Cincinnati: Servant Books, 2001), 115.

What is important for all Christians to understand is that God's call extends to the whole of a Christian's life. No part is excluded. This is what Luther called, "the priesthood of all believers." All baptized and believing Christians have a priestly status before God. By this, Luther did not mean to denigrate the office or spiritual authority of the clergy. Luther simply wanted the Church to understand that our mission, our vocation as Christians, includes both being part of what God is doing in the Church to create and sustain faith, and what God is doing in the world to sustain justice and life.

Finding Our Vocation: "Condemnation, Conformation, or Creation?"

Our calling is to use our God-given gifts and talents to further God's purposes in *all areas of human endeavor.* God has a purpose for humanity. There is a God-given purpose for the Church, but also for the world of business, politics, education, agriculture, science, medicine, and the arts. Each of us must discern God's call for our lives and God gives us a lot of freedom to choose. There are many different vocations, but what matters is that we align our lives with the "divine intentionality."[124]

Christians are called into the world in order to be part of God's creative purposes, not mindlessly to condemn or copy the world.[125] To condemn or copy are relatively easy. Christians are called to create. This is much more difficult. Our calling is to be artists who, however imperfectly in this sinful world, seek to create something beautiful to God's glory.

---

124. The obvious question the reader may ask is, "What does God want *me* to do?" How do we discern our personal vocation? Let me recommend here Robert Benne's succinct and wise discussion of this question in *Ordinary Saints: An Introduction to the Christian Life* (Minneapolis: Fortress, 2003), 104-108.

125. Andy Crouch, *Culture Making: Recovering Our Creative Calling* (Downers Grove, IL: IVP Books, 2008), 65-77.

Some Christians specialize in condemnation. They reason that since the world is going to hell in the proverbial hand-basket, the best way to live is to separate ourselves from it. We retreat into a Christian subculture that does not engage the world. Let's hunker down and wait for Jesus to come back. This attitude is what gives rise to all the books and movies about the End Times. If the world is lost, the goal of the Christian is simply not to be *Left Behind*. In this scheme, the Christian hope is to escape from planet Earth.[126]

On the other hand, many Christians make the counter move. We must be "relevant" to the world. Yet nothing is so short-lived as relevance. There's something amiss when Christians seek to mimic the music, mindset, and mores of the world. We may tell ourselves that we do this in order to reach the world, but subtly we begin to seek the world's favor and approval. Worship becomes entertainment. Evangelism becomes social action. Preaching mimics pop psychology. Morality mirrors Hollywood. Slowly, perhaps imperceptibly, the Christian witness is compromised.

There's a healthier, more faithful, option. The Church at her best has rejected both blanket condemnation and mindless compromise. The Church lived *faithfully and creatively* in the world.

It's hard to imagine, but there was a time when Christians were at the forefront of cultural creativity. Many of the greatest artists, poets, writers, musicians, scientists, authors, politicians, and social reformers were people motivated and inspired by their Christian sense of calling. We may not have the gifts of a St. Benedict, or a Galileo, or a Michelangelo, or a Bach, or a Dorothy Day, or a Mother Teresa; but with them we are called creatively to bring the light of Christ into the darkness and

---

126. For the classic treatment of how Christians have understood their relationships to the wider cultures, see H. Richard Niebuhr, *Christ and Culture* (New York: Harper and Row, 1951, First Harper Colophon Edition, 1975).

decay of the world. We are called to conserve the best of culture and to create new possibilities. We are "the salt and light of the world" God loves. The call of God to all Christians is a call to create something beautiful in our own historically particular time and place.

God's call extends over the entirety of our particular lives. However, there are four areas of life in which hearing God's call is crucial: Work, Citizenship, Church, and Family.

Work

In the summer before my senior year of high school, I got a job in a factory which made Recreational Vehicles. I worked on an assembly line assembling the grill on the front end of these large, expensive motor homes. It was hot, hectic, and I hated it. My bosses didn't care if our work was slipshod. I was never fast enough. It just needed to "look" good. What mattered was that at the end of the day there was a certain number of shiny new vehicles ready for sale. I feel sorry for the people who paid good money for those RVs which I helped to make.

Earlier we saw how Luther tried to instill dignity into the daily work of ordinary people. He insisted that "the humble milkmaid does more for the kingdom than a monk in his cell."[127] It's easy for Lutherans and other Protestants to quote Luther with an attitude of theological superiority. We "know" that God is more pleased with daily tasks performed with Christian faith and love than with self-chosen religious works of the pious locked in their convents and monasteries. So there!

What we too easily forget is historical context. Luther's worldview was fully sacramental. God's presence permeated creation and life. Human beings were co-creators with the Creator. Luther rightly wanted all life to be lived in a kind of Eucharistic adoration. Christ was *ubiquitously* present. Creation itself was a sacrament. God was present and glorified in each

---

127. Robert Benne, *Ordinary Saints*, 171.

creative task performed in cooperation with the divine intentionality. The milkmaid's task was, so to speak, to squeeze sweetness from the udder of life given though a cow. A joyous task indeed!

However, Luther's sacramental world is now thoroughly "disenchanted." The vast majority of people in our postmodern world work without any sense of the sacred being served. God is no longer the One before whom we live and work. When God is absent, work easily becomes a daily drudgery which offers little personal satisfaction. The bottom line is not God's glory, but profit margins and paying the bills.

What we've failed to realize is that Luther wanted the milk stall to become like the monk's stall — a place of prayer and service. Our Post-Reformation situation is not improved if God is removed from both stalls. The whole earth is to be a monastery.

One of the greatest gifts Christians can offer the world is to re-enchant the workplace as a sacramental space. Certainly, the realities of a fallen world will make this challenging. Work cannot always be fun or rewarding. Work is hard. But any work done for the purpose of re-enchanting the world with God's loving presence and purpose is greatly fulfilling.

Citizenship

The late Father Richard Neuhaus once wrote, "When I meet God, I expect to meet him as an American." He meant that each of us lives out our lives within a concrete cultural context. If you're reading this, then you're probably an American. If not, then when you meet God you will meet Him as the "culturally corporeal" creature you are. No one reading this will meet God as a citizen of Nazi Germany or the Ming Dynasty. We are called to live as disciples of Christ within the historical particularity of our own time and place. Fr. Neuhaus went on to clarify:

> Not most importantly as an American, to be sure, but as someone who tried to take seriously, and tried to en-

courage others to take seriously, the story of America within the story of the world. The argument, in short, is that God is not indifferent toward the American experiment, and therefore we who are *called* (emphasis added) to think about God and his ways through time dare not be indifferent to the American experiment.[128]

God is not "indifferent" to any part of this world, and the American experiment has had a major and lasting impact on the story of the world. How do we as citizens of both America (or any other nation) and the Kingdom of God live out our responsibilities? In other words, how do we, "Render to Caesar the things that are Caesar's, and to God the things that are God's"?[129]

We shouldn't fool ourselves into thinking this will be easy. Just wrap the cross with the flag and love both? Mindless patriotism gets both God and country wrong.

The world is a messy place. God's perfect will is, unfortunately, not yet done on earth as in heaven. Still, we must try to do what we can *as Christians and as Americans* to make God's justice and peace a reality in the world.

In 2009-2010 our two sons were both deployed — one to Iraq and one to Afghanistan. Nothing prepared me for this. As a Christian, I had deep reservations about the justness of these wars. As an American, I was proud of our sons knowing that they were both young men of integrity who truly wanted to be on the side of the angels. I was caught in an emotional, moral, and theological quandary.

What I learned through this experience is that there are no utopian solutions to living as a Christian and an American. Everything falls short of God's kingdom. However, Christians

---

128. Richard John Neuhaus, *Time toward Home*, as quoted by Randy Boyagoda, *Richard John Neuhaus: A Life in the Public Square* (New York: Image, 2015), 383.

129. Luke 20:25.

can look at the hard facts of life, all the horrors and ambiguities of history, knowing that ultimately God's will, will be done. We live and work with a "certain hope" and with the "ache of longing" for God's kingdom to come. In the interim, we do what we can as we try to discern our vocations. Seeking in small but real ways, to live faithfully and to try to make God's promised future reign present in the here and now. This is our calling. I also expect to meet God as an American.

Church

In the last chapter of this book, we'll think more deeply about our calling to be members of the Church, the Body of Christ. Here we need simply to note that *every* Christian is *called* to be part of the Church. There are no exceptions. We all know "Christians" who have no serious commitment to the local church. In doing so, they rob the Church of their gifts.

The Roman Catholic Church teaches that the purposeful refusal to attend mass is a "mortal" sin. This means that the willful neglect of participation and reception of the Word and Sacrament is spiritually deadening. Protestants have shied away from this because it can lead to a certain legalism in which "showing up at mass" is something to check off the list of good deeds done for the week.

However, there is also something right about this idea. It really is "mortally" wounding to faith when we separate ourselves from hearing God's Word and receiving God's sacraments. Faith needs to be fed or it will grow weak. Faith can even die. Where there is no faith, there are no works of faith. And, "Faith without works is dead."[130]

We can doubt or question some callings. Is God calling me to marry? Is God calling me to the mission field? Etc. But you can have no doubt, God is calling you to be an active member in a Christian church.

---

130. James 2:26.

Marriage and Family

Finally, we come to vocations of marriage and family. Most of us will live out our Christian vocations within the context of a family. We're not disembodied spirits, we're flesh-and-blood human beings. Marriage and raising children are all God-given vocations. As mentioned, there was a time within Roman Catholicism, when these vocations were viewed as allowances for the weak. The higher and better call was to celibacy.

It's important, especially for Protestants, not to dismiss the importance of celibacy in the life of the Church. It is a high and holy calling by which some forfeit family life in order to fulfill their God's call. There are situations where marriage and family would be hindrances to a vocation.

That said, there is also a high and holy calling to marriage and family life. Marriage is not just a "permitted" way of life allowed for those who can't control their sexual desires. Rather, marriage is a calling to create a sacramental reflection of the intimacy between the Church and Christ (Bride and Groom). It is also the call to procreate. Children are gifts from God.[131]

Marriage and Divorce

If you believe our liturgies,
no marriage may be sundered,
but lawyers say six-figure fees
can fix what God has blundered.

— "Revisionism" by A.M. Juster

If marriage is a lifelong calling, then it is certain that we don't always listen to that call. Divorce is rampant in our society. There are few if any people reading this whose lives have not been touched by marital breakup. Among the general population in this country, approximately 50 percent of all marriages

---

131. Many couples struggle with infertility. To desire the gift of children, and to be unable to conceive is a painful reality for many couples.

end in divorce. For many people today, including many Christians, divorce is "no big deal." How do we as Christians seeking to live faithfully under the call of God respond to this crisis?

In the past, there was a broad consensus among all of the churches — Protestant, Catholic, and Orthodox — regarding marriage and family life. The Christian consensus said that marriage is a life-long covenant between a man and a woman. Marriage was the "rightly ordered" relationship for the expression of sexual intimacy. Children were seen as the fruit of marital intimacy, gifts from God.[132] It was, of course, always acknowledged that because of sin, human beings frequently fell short of this ideal. As sinful human beings, all of us fall short of the ideal.[133] When people fall short, the way forward was, and still is, through repentance and the grace of forgiveness. God offers us a new start.

However, even God's forgiveness does not undo the pain caused by marital shipwrecks. Real people, often including children, get hurt and live with the emotional scars of divorce.

It's true that some marriages need to end. For example, when there is adultery, abandonment, or abuse, then the injured party may with good conscience choose to end the marriage (cf. Matthew 5:31-32; I Corinthians 7:10ff.). However,

---

132. Because sexual intimacy has a twofold purpose — the unitive ("the two shall be one") and the procreative ("be fruitful and multiply") — most Protestants (and some Orthodox) believe that it is not necessary that intercourse "always" be open to procreation. The Roman Catholic Church would disagree with this and insist that sexual intercourse must always be open to life — hence *natural family planning*. It is interesting to note that recently some Protestants are reexamining their stance on this issue. For a Protestant reassessment of artificial contraception see *Open Embrace: A Protestant Couple Rethinks Contraception* by Sam and Bethany Torode (Grand Rapids: Eerdmans, 2002). For our purposes, let's simply say that the *responsible* use of artificial birth control (which does not destroy a developing human fetus) is left to the conscience of married couples. Abortion as a means of birth control is wholly rejected.

133. Matthew 5:27-28.

divorce is *always* a tragic *and sinful* rending of what God has meant to be a lifelong, loving, covenantal relationship. As someone once said, "There are two things that should *never* be entered into prematurely: embalming and divorce." That divorce is rather commonplace, even among Christians, scandalizes Jesus' clear teaching about the indissolubility of marriage.[134] It is a very big deal indeed.

A word here also needs to be said about those for whom marriage is not possible. Can singleness be a calling? Here, Protestants can learn from Roman Catholics that it is possible for people to live full and happy lives without marriage and family. Even, as impossible as it may seem to be in our sex-saturated society, without sex! To be sure, the single life has its own unique challenges. To live a chaste life in singleness is not easy, and most people desire to share their lives with a spouse and to have children. As a pastor, I often speak with single people who share their feelings of loneliness and the desire to be married. I also see single people heroically remaining chaste when society keeps telling them that it is unnatural not to fulfill their sexual desires. At the same time, the single life can offer people some unique opportunities and rewards. Often, singleness creates opportunities for service and adventure that are denied those who have the responsibilities associated with marriage and the rearing of children. For some — and this will always be a minority — the single life *is* a calling from God.

A Word about Homosexuality and Same Sex "Marriage"[135]

We now come to a very difficult issue for Christians. The question with which many are wrestling today is whether or not

---

134. Matthew 19:1-12; Mark 10:1-12.

135. For a brief, balanced introduction to the current debate, see *Homosexuality and the Bible: Two Views* by Robert A. J. Gagnon and Dan O. Via (Minneapolis: Augsburg Fortress, 2003).

homosexual couples can be sexually intimate as a *vocation of God* and therefore be married in the Church. The question Christians ask is: "What kinds of sexually intimate unions can the Church publicly and officially bless?" Is homosexuality a calling of the Spirit or is it a disordered calling of the flesh that must be resisted and which must never be blessed by the Church? If heterosexuals experience their calling to marriage at least in part through their innate sexual attractions, are homosexuals experiencing a call through their same-sex attractions?[136]

Many of the current debates and divisions over homosexuality arise in the Church when trying to balance two concerns: 1) the authority of the Bible as it has historically been interpreted, and 2) the experience of people who know and love homosexuals, and who see the goodness, creativity, and *Christian faith* of many gays and lesbians.

As we saw earlier, Christianity emphasizes the authority of the Bible in all matters of faith and practice. The Bible *is* God's written word. The Holy Spirit speaks anew through these ancient texts. However, as Kathryn Greene-McCreight so wisely states: "The Holy Spirit speaks today, yes, but never in contradiction or dissonance to Scripture."[137] What God has said in the past is valid even if unpopular.

Also, the authority of the Bible is not a matter of personal, individualistic interpretation (remember the "rule of faith"). Rather, we must read and understand the Bible as it has been *historically and universally understood and interpreted by the Church.*[138] My personal interpretation of the Bible should echo the thought and theology of God's people through time. All

---

136. As of June, 2015, by a 5/4 decision of the U.S. Supreme Court, gay "marriage" is now the law of the land.

137. Kathryn Greene-McCreight, "He Spoke Through the Prophets," in *Nicene Christianity: The Future for a New Ecumenism,* ed. Christopher R. Seitz (Grand Rapids: Brazos Press, 2001), 174.

138. This is true of evangelical Protestants, magisterial Protestants in mainline churches, Roman Catholics, and the Orthodox.

faithful interpretations should complement, and not contradict, the witness of the communion of saints throughout history.

Protestant Christians place particular stress on the authority of Scripture and believe that the final (not only) authority in all matters of faith, teaching, and practice is the Bible. So what does the Bible say about homosexual behavior? The Bible's prohibition against homosexual acts is fairly clear (Leviticus 18:22; Romans 1:24ff.; I Corinthians 6:9-10; I Timothy 1:10). Even more importantly and more clearly stated are the Bible's affirmation of heterosexual marriage which God instituted *before* the Fall (Genesis 2).[139] According to the Bible, the complementary nature of the sexes is woven into God's creative plan and purpose (Genesis 1). It is part of the natural law. Jesus endorsed the same traditional biblical understanding of heterosexual marriage (Matthew 19:1-12; Mark 10:1-12; Luke 19:1-12).

However, other committed Christians speak from their experiences of knowing and loving homosexuals or of their own personal struggles with homoerotic attractions. These Christians often emphasize the fact that just as the early Church wrestled with the question of the inclusion of the Gentiles, so we wrestle today with the inclusion of homosexuals. The early Church came to see that God willed to embrace *all* humanity through Christ (Jew and Gentile). This conclusion was reached because Jews saw God's call verified when Gentiles received the Holy Spirit, proving they indeed were accepted by God.[140] Christians who believe in the full inclusion (including marriage) of homosexuals argue that many homosexual people give evidence of having received the Holy Spirit. Who are we to reject those whom God has accepted? Furthermore, these Christians

---

139. Cf. John Stott, "Homosexual Partnerships?" in *Involvement Volume II: Social and Sexual Relationships in the Modern World, A Crucial Questions Book* (Old Tappan, NJ: Fleming H. Revell, 1984, 1985), 215-244.

140. Acts 10:44-48 and 11:1ff.

111

rightly argue that our sexual identity does not supersede our baptismal identity as God's children.

Critics of this line of reasoning note that the issue is not the inclusion of homosexuals into the Church. The Church welcomes all people, but the Bible exhorts members of the Church to abstain from various sexual practices and behaviors: fornication, adultery, and homoerotic intercourse. Gentiles received into the Church *were* required to abstain from sexual immorality (*porneia* — Acts 15:29).

So, we have a problem. A problem that will not be resolved to everyone's liking in this book. But let me speak as a person who knows and cares about homosexual people, and who is also deeply committed to the authority of the Bible and the catholic faith.

First, the biblical witness against homosexual practice is persuasive. No "hermeneutical"[141] sleight of hand can change the obvious. No individual Christian or Christian denomination has the authority to compromise a clear and consistent teaching of the Bible. Christians are part of a tradition of biblical interpretation that stretches back thousands of years. The Holy Spirit did not leave the Church after the last page of the New Testament was written. We must listen to the collective theological and ethical wisdom of the Church across time. When we do so, we discover that there is a clear and consistent teaching on issues of sexual ethics. This "authoritative" teaching is still held by the vast majority of Christians (and non-Christians) throughout the world.[142]

---

141. Hermeneutics is the branch of theology dealing with how biblical texts are interpreted.

142. A minority of Christians, especially in Europe and America, disagree. They say that we must give up the idea of an authoritative tradition of biblical interpretation. This "authoritative tradition" only gives voice to the victors in the Church's theological struggles. Instead they argue that we must listen to the voices of the oppressed — including the sexual oppressed minorities like homosexuals who are often unrepresented or

When we listen to God's Word in Scripture and echoed in the teaching of the Church, we hear of the importance of heterosexual marriage as sacramentally reflective of the mystery of Christ's relationship with His Bride, the Church (Ephesians 5). When we read the Bible *with* the Church, we are led to the unavoidable conclusion that heterosexual marriage is the only sexually intimate relationship the Church can bless.[143] This is difficult to write because I do not want to add pain to my friends and family members who identify themselves as homosexual, some of whom are in committed, monogamous sexual relationships. Often these relationships, like many heterosexual marriages, reflect a measure of true goodness and grace. This, it seems to me, suggests that God's grace and goodness are larger than human sinfulness. Nevertheless, the Church cannot bless sinfulness, but can and must bless the sinner. We cannot bless brokenness, but we can and must bless, love, and heal the broken.

Second, within the Christian Church of every tradition and denomination for two millennia, all have agreed that marriage is always between one man and one woman. This is not only affirmed by the Scriptures, but again, by natural law. It is rather

---

misrepresented in the Bible. Of course, the problem is that once the Bible is viewed as only the "voice of the victor," then it ceases to be a theologically and morally compelling narrative. The Church has always insisted that the Victor's Voice we hear echoing in Scripture is the Voice of God. The Voice of God is frequently unpopular, but it must be heard.

143. Some Protestants reading this may object by saying that the *sola scriptura* principle disallows for any authoritative tradition. The Bible alone is enough. However, as the Lutheran theologian Robert Benne noted after the decision by the Evangelical Lutheran Church in America to allow for ordination of active homosexuals and for the blessing of same-sex unions in its congregations: "*Sola Scriptura* ... did not seem to be sufficient ... an authoritative tradition of interpretation of the Bible seemed to be essential. More was needed than the Bible alone. Protestants seem to lack such an authoritative tradition, so the fight and split" (christianitytoday.com, "How the ELCA Left the Great Tradition for Liberal Protestantism," September 14, 2009).

obvious that male and female are natural and complementary counterparts. Scripture, Church, and natural law all agree.

Finally, having acknowledged the authority of the witness of Scripture, Church, and nature, the truth is we *all* struggle with various besetting sins, behaviors, attitudes, and desires that we cannot fully understand or control. This is true of sexual desires, but also of other kinds of "disordered" affections and desires (food, alcohol, money, etc.). God, fortunately, still accepts us and grants us the Holy Spirit even though none of us lives in perfect obedience to God's will. It is most instructive that after Paul has written his strongest words against homosexual behavior, he immediately writes:

> You, therefore, have no excuse, you who pass judgment on someone else, for at whatever point you judge the other, you are condemning yourself, because you who pass judgment do the same things.[144]

While it is clear that St. Paul looked negatively on homosexual behavior, we should always keep in mind that he also looked just as negatively on many other behaviors *and attitudes*—greed, gossip, selfishness, pride, envy, jealousy, drunkenness, idolatry, lust, fornication (premarital sex) and adultery (extramarital sex). Does anyone "not" see themselves somewhere in that list of vice? Ephraim Radner wisely cautions against singling out homosexuality as the target of condemnation:

> If heterosexual Christians condemn gay people for their homosexual acts, they inevitably condemn themselves even more so (for their own pride, arrogance, lack of love, etc.). The point here is not that what is right in God's eyes is unknown, but that what is wrong in human eyes is obscured by self-righteousness.[145]

---

144. Romans 2:1.

145. Ephraim Radner, *Hope Among the Fragments: The Broken Church and Its Engagement of Scripture* (Grand Rapids: Brazos Press, 2004), 148.

Faithfulness to the Bible as God's written Word, to the Word of God incarnate in Jesus, and the teaching of the Church catholic, will help us to navigate safely between the Scylla of self-righteousness and the Charybdis of unrighteousness.

I told you that I would not resolve this to everyone's liking. However, if I were trying to please people, "I would not be a servant of Christ."[146]

---

146. Galatians 1:10.

Questions for Discussion

1. Do you think that you have "messed up" God's plan for your life?

2. What is the difference between God having a plan and God having a purpose for everyone?

3. Briefly outline the Roman Catholic and Protestant distortions of the concept of call.

4. What is the difference between having a vocation and having a job?

5. Are there some "jobs" that God would never call us to take?

6. How have you experienced God's call? If so, how, when, what were you called to do?

7. Do you agree with the traditional Christian view of marriage? Why or why not?

8. What do you think about the view of homosexuality presented here?

9. What does it mean to steer clear of the "Scylla of legalism and the Charybdis of antinomianism"?

10. What is the difference between making a moral judgment and being judgmental?

Chapter 6

What If Resurrection Is Our Destiny?

Who would fardels [burdens] bear
To grunt and sweat under a weary life,
But that the dread of something after death,
The undiscovered country from whose bourn
No traveler returns, puzzles the will
And makes us rather bear those ills we have
Than fly to others that we know not of?
— Shakespeare, Hamlet

Love, evil, the union of body and soul, and death are
examples of mysteries. Mathematics, tree surgery, and
butterfly collecting are examples of problems. —Peter Kreeft

During the summer of my sixth year my life changed forever. My strong and loving father went to work one day and was killed in an accident. I have vivid memories of my grandfather rushing into the house in a panic to get me and my older brother and sister. For several days we stayed with relatives as dad lay in a hospital. Three days later, my dad died at the age of forty-one.

I remember going to the funeral home to view him. It was the first time I'd seen a dead body. My aunt showed me a dark, bruised place on his face still evident even after the mortician's attempts to cover it with cosmetics. My mother fainted, and I remember thinking to myself, "no more daddy."

117

We live in a world filled to overflowing with grief. Almost everyone who reads this is grieving some loss. I've spent over thirty years as a pastor, and know that I am always preaching to a congregation of mourners. Not only do we mourn the dead, we fear death. To be human is to learn to live with the certainty of death. All of us think about — and maybe even lose sleep worrying about — the fact of death and what may lie beyond. There is a reason why *Ghost Hunters* and other television shows dealing with the paranormal are such commercial successes. We want some evidence for life after death to assuage our fear. We want certainty to our faith. Many people turn to religion in order to gain that certainty. We don't like uncertainty and ambiguity. Unfortunately any discussion of life after death is fraught with both.

There's only one certain thing. We all will die. Some Christians may try to avoid this unpleasant truth with hopes of a soon-to-be Rapture in which we gain glory without the cross. But such theologies are built more on the sand of wishful thinking rather than serious theological study. So, stop reading and consider this, *you* will die. And please don't try to bring in some pious nonsense about living on in the memories of others or our children. They will die too. Either there is life with God afterwards or there isn't. On this, we can all agree.

Writing with Blood, Sweat, and Tears

Writing and talking about heaven and the hereafter is relatively easy as long as it is treated as an academic exercise. We can speculate about and ponder the mysteries of the hereafter from the relative safe confines of the here-and-now. We can air our dogmatic certainties to each other. However, things radically change when we move from theological or philosophical speculation to existential event.

We should do our thinking and writing and talking about death in cancer wards and with hospice patients. Then we'd have a reminder of what's at stake in the discussion. Anti-religious bigots who lampoon the simple believer as intellectually

118

challenged and religious fundamentalists who exude a saccharine certainty about both the landscape and the population of heaven (and hell) should rein in their rhetoric. Let's be honest: We all see in a mirror dimly.[147]

Joseph Sittler, a pastor and a theologian, tells a story about a dear lady who came to him soon after the death of her husband. She began to pour out her grief and said:

> ...it's particularly hard late in the afternoon sitting at the window watching where he used to come around the corner in summertime, his coat over his arm, slapping his leg with the evening paper. He always stopped just when he thought I couldn't see him and knocked out his pipe. He knew I didn't want him to smoke so much, although I kept sewing up the burnt holes in his coat pockets. That time of day is a terrible one for me to get through, because I know he won't come around the corner any more. In heaven do you suppose he and I will live together in a cottage with a white fence?[148]

Certainly this dear woman's faith is heartwarming, and her grief is heart-rending. But is her hope of heaven in a "cottage with a white fence" true to the Christian vision? Is heaven simply the good of earth exponentially increased? When the description of heaven takes on too much detail, we begin to suspect that someone is only trying to make us feel better. Heaven soon becomes less a reality and more an escape from reality.

Turning to the Bible, we find the biblical writers are wise enough *not* to say too much about heaven. Paul summarizes the biblical hope best in Romans 14:8 where he writes: "If we live, we live to the Lord, and if we die, we die to the Lord; so then, whether we live or whether we die, we are the Lord's." That's it. There are no specifics given. No chubby

---

147. I Corinthians 13:12.

148. Joseph Sittler, *Gravity and Grace: Reflections and Provocations* (Minneapolis: Augsburg, 1986), 125-126.

cherubs, no pearly gates, no St. Peter waiting to give us an entrance exam. This is about as concrete as the Bible gets concerning heaven.

We should also note that "heaven" is often a shorthand way of referring to God's future. The Christian hope is not that we will exist eternally in a spiritual, disembodied state. The hope is resurrection. Throughout the Bible there is a strong and persistent promise that God's future means a "new heaven and a new earth."[149] The biblical hope and promise is what N.T. Wright calls, "Life after life after death."[150] We'll think more about this in the next chapter. What must be emphasized here is that the Christian hope is that nature as we know it will not be abandoned by God, but transformed by God's power into "supernaturalized nature."[151] St. Paul tries to get at this mystery when he writes, "It is sown a natural body, it is raised a spiritual body."[152] Perhaps the resurrected body will be comprised purely of "quarks" or some other weird form of matter/energy. Who knows?

The Resurrection of Jesus Christ

The Resurrection of Jesus is our best peek into what God has in store for us and all creation. Jesus' resurrected body was "supernaturalized." All the biblical witnesses tell us that his resurrected body was both tangible (natural) and spiritual (supernatural). His Resurrection was the "first fruits" of what God has in store for those who belong to Him.[153] Therefore, what he is, we shall also be.

---

149. Revelation 21.

150. N.T. Wright, *Surprised by Hope: Rethinking Heaven, the Resurrection, and the Mission of the Church* (New York: Harper One, 2008), 148ff.

151. Terrence Nichols, *Death and Afterlife: A Theological Introduction* (Grand Rapids: Brazos, 2010), 144.

152. I Corinthians 15:44a.

153. I Corinthians 15:20.

It's very important to understand that all Christian thinking about these issues is grounded in the fact that Jesus Christ, the crucified one, truly rose from the dead. Our hope is completely based upon this truth. The Resurrection of Jesus is the center, source, and summit of the Christian faith. If the Resurrection never happened, the Christian faith is a sham. As Paul so wisely wrote in the New Testament that if Christ has not been raised from the dead, we Christians are "of all people most to be pitied."[154]

However, there are many good historical reasons to accept the witness of the Bible to the fact of Jesus' resurrection. Interested readers are urged to read more deeply on this subject.[155] Here, I'll only mention one very ordinary event which helped me.

I was taking the required undergraduate course in Western Civilization. The Professor was both learned and engaging. One day in class, as we studied the rise of Christianity as a historical event, he said: "The real question you must ask yourself is what made the disciples of Jesus believe he rose from the dead." I'll never forget that moment. Historically, it is indisputable that the earliest disciples of Jesus believed that their crucified Master had been raised. They believed it enough to die for it. As Pascal noted in the 17th century, the disciples were either "deceived or deceivers." I could not, and cannot, believe that the witnesses behind the New Testament were deceivers. Nor can I believe that they were simply duped into faith. Their witness is too gracious and good. They believed it. The fundamental question is whether or not we believe their witness. Everything else is detail.

At the Border of the Undiscovered Country: Near Death Experiences

I said earlier that we should do our thinking and writing about death in places where we are forced to confront the reality of

---

154. I Corinthians 15:19.

155. For an exhaustive study of the historical evidence see *The Resurrection of the Son of God* by N.T. Wright (Minneapolis: Fortress, 2003).

death. Consequently, it seems sensible to pay attention to those who have come closer to the Undiscovered Country than most of us have.

Ever since Dr. Raymond Moody published his best-selling study of people who had "died" and been brought back, the literature on near-death experiences (NDEs) keeps growing.[156] All of us have heard and read stories of these experiences. Some are quite convincing — *if* you are inclined to believe.[157]

While I personally try to keep both an open mind and a skeptical disposition, some of these stories may help us to better see the reality of the post-mortem world. It is important to remember that our faith does not rest on the truth or falsity of these experiences. Our faith rests on the foundation of God's grace made concrete in the resurrection of our Lord Jesus Christ.

With that caveat, let's look at one of the more remarkable and believable NDEs of which I am aware. It is the experience of Richard John Neuhaus who was for 30 years a Lutheran pastor and theologian. In the early 1990s Pastor Neuhaus became Father Neuhaus when he entered into full communion with the Roman Catholic Church. He was a respected person of faith on both sides of the Church aisle (Catholic and Protestant). He was well-known for his wit and wisdom, but was certainly not given to flights of fancy. He had a near death experience.

Father Neuhaus' experience began with an ordinary stomachache. He visited his doctor who ordered a colonoscopy. The colonoscopy revealed nothing unusual. However, there was no relief from the abdominal pains. Then on Sunday afternoon, January 10, 1993, the pain became unbearable and he was rushed to the hospital. He describes the pain as feeling that his "stomach was exploding."[158]

---

156. Raymond Moody, *Life after Life* (New York: Bantam, 1975, 1981).

157. For a fair assessment of the evidence see Dinesh D'Souza, *Life After Death: The Evidence* (Regnery Publishing, 2009) especially pages 53-72.

158. For the complete article see, Richard John Neuhaus, "As I Lay Dying," *First Things* (February, 2000).

At the hospital, the doctor on duty ordered an x-ray that revealed a large tumor. The tumor had grown and ruptured the intestine, causing "blood, fecal matter, and guts" to poison his system. After an emergency surgery which sliced his stomach "from the rib cage to the pubic area," he was sewed up. All that could be done now was to wait and pray. Then the hemorrhaging began, and the doctors did not know what was causing it. His blood pressure collapsed. What to do? Could he survive another surgery? Without surgery he was certain to die from the hemorrhaging. So they opened him up again.

Father Neuhaus survived the second surgery and was recovering in the ICU. This alone was perhaps miraculous, but the remarkable part of his experience occurred a few days after leaving the ICU. The following is lengthy, but it's important to let Father Neuhaus tell the experience in his own words:

> It was a couple of days after leaving intensive care, and it was night. I could hear patients in adjoining rooms moaning and mumbling and occasionally calling out; the surrounding medical machines were pumping and sucking and bleeping as usual. Then, all of a sudden, I was jerked into an utterly lucid state of awareness. I was sitting up in the bed staring intently into the darkness, although in fact I knew my body was lying flat. What I was staring at was a color like blue and purple, and vaguely in the form of hanging drapery. By the drapery were two "presences." I saw them and yet did not see them, and I cannot explain that. But they were there, and I knew that I was not tied to the bed. I was able and prepared to get up and go somewhere. And then the presences — one or both of them, I do not know — spoke. This I heard clearly. Not in an ordinary way, for I cannot remember anything about the voice. But the message was beyond mistaking: "Everything is ready now."

> That was it. They waited for a while, maybe for a minute. Whether they were waiting for a response or just waiting to see whether I had received the message, I don't know.

123

"Everything is ready now." It was not in the form of a command, nor was it an invitation to do anything. They were just letting me know. Then they were gone, and I was again flat on my back with my mind racing wildly. I had an iron resolve to determine right then and there what had happened. Had I been dreaming? In no way. I was then and was now as lucid and wide awake as I had ever been in my life.

Tell me that I was dreaming and you might as well tell me that I was dreaming that I wrote the sentence before this one. Testing my awareness, I pinched myself hard, and ran through the multiplication tables, and recalled the birth dates of my seven brothers and sisters, and my wits were vibrantly about me. The whole thing had lasted three or four minutes, maybe less. I resolved at that moment that I would never, never let anything dissuade me from the reality of what had happened.

Fortunately for us, Father Neuhaus survived to tell his story.[159] What I find most intriguing is the clarity, the honesty, and the uniqueness of this NDE. Father Neuhaus does not say that he was swept into a tunnel toward a Light, which seems to be common in such experiences. He does not claim too much nor give excessive details. Yet, he possessed a remarkable mental clarity throughout the experience. The unbeliever will undoubtedly dismiss this as a phenomena brought on by a lack of oxygen to the brain or too many pain medications. They may be right. But they may be wrong.

If we take Father Neuhaus' experience at face value — or faith value — we have here a credible account of an experience of the paranormal. *If* this is indeed what it was, then it is an intriguing "glimpse" into the Undiscovered Country.

---

159. Fr. Richard Neuhaus had this near death experience on January 20, 1993, and died 15 years later on January 8, 2009.

The Resurrection of the Body and the Immortality of the Soul

One question that many believers ask about the afterlife concerns the relationship between the resurrection of the body and the immortality of the soul. It may come as a surprise to some, but the Christian Church does not (strictly speaking) believe in the immortality of the soul. Only God is immortal; the existence of all other beings is contingent upon God's will. My existence right now as I think these thoughts and type these words is a gift from God. Any existence after my physical death is also a gift from God. In other words, as the German theologian Helmut Thielicke says, "Our real immortality is nothing but another expression for the faithfulness of God, which is stronger than death and will never put our trust to shame."[160]

The Greek philosopher Plato probably taught the idea of a *natural immortality* of the soul, and he greatly influenced later Jewish and Christian thinkers. For Plato and many others past and present, a human being is innately immortal *even if* God does not exist! This would be an absurdity to the writers of the Bible. Raymond Anderson helps us understand the issue when he writes, "What is at stake is not the belief that there is life after death but whether that life is due to something resident in human nature or whether it is due to God's power and Spirit."[161] In other words, when Christians speak of "the immortality of the soul," this should not be understood to mean that human beings possess an immortal spirit trapped in a mortal body like a "ghost in a machine." Life here on Earth, and life in Heaven are both dependent on the gracious will of a gracious God.

---

160. Helmut Thielicke, *How the World Began: Man in the First Chapters of the Bible*, trans. by John W. Doberstein (Philadelphia: Muhlenberg Press, second printing 1961), 249.

161. Raymond Anderson, "On Being Human: The Spiritual Saga of a Creaturely Soul," in *Whatever Happened to the Soul?* ed. by Warren S. Brown, Nancey Murphy and H. Newton Malony (Minneapolis: Fortress Press, 1998), 192.

According to the Christian understanding, a human being is an "enfleshed" soul. But what exactly does that mean? Peter Kreeft is helpful here. This can be a little difficult, but take some time with it, read it slowly, and think about it:

> ...the body is in the soul, not the soul in the body....The soul carries its body with it. When death separates the two, we have a freak, a monster, an obscenity. That is why we are terrified of ghosts and corpses, though both are harmless: they are obscenely separated aspects of what belongs together as one.[162]

Whatever does this mean? Kreeft explains:

> ...body is form. Even now what makes our bodies our bodies is not atoms but structure. The atoms change every seven years; yet it is the same body because of its continuity of form.... It is like a river. A river is not its water, which is always moving on, but its riverbed, which forms the formless water into a river.[163]

This analogy is very helpful. The body, your physical fleshly body, is like the water in a river. The water changes as it moves along. You cannot step into the same river twice. The riverbed "forms" the river like your soul "forms" your physical body. Your soul forms or "informs" your body giving it pattern, direction, depth, shallowness, etc.

Your immortal soul is "informing" your mortal fleshly body. Your flesh is not resurrected. The flesh will decompose and be eaten by "worms, fish, and fisherman."[164] Your soul (*psyche*) — your will, thoughts, attitudes, feelings, imaginings, loves, desires, memories, personality, hatreds, etc. — right now informs your body. Our souls shape our lives like the riverbed shapes the river. Your body is *in* your soul like water is *in* a riverbed.

---

162. Peter Kreeft, *Every Thing You Ever Wanted to Know About Heaven: But Never Dreamed of Asking* (San Francisco: Ignatius, 1990), 92-93.
163. Ibid.95.
164. Ibid.96.

When the body dies, the soul leaves the body just like water evaporates when it is no longer held within the confines of the riverbed. "Once the form (soul) departs, this unity: atoms, molecules, tissues, and organs of the body begin to disintegrate and scatter."[165] In the Resurrection, when the soul is united to a "spiritual body,"[166] the resurrected body will also (just like the physical body) be informed by the soul.

Is There an Intermediate State between Death and Resurrection?

So we may ask, what happens to the soul once it leaves the body? In other words, to keep with the previous analogy, what happens to the river bed when the river dries up? The riverbed remains, but it is obvious that something vital is missing -- the water. The riverbed "longs" to be filled with the river. So the soul longs to be clothed with a body. The soul feels empty or "naked" without the body.[167] The Old Testament calls this "intermediate" state of the soul the shadowy existence in "Sheol." It is not that the soul ceases to exist at death, but it ceases to be fully alive until God gives the soul a "spiritual" or "resurrected" body like a river is "resurrected" by the rain.[168] But how can we conceive or imagine this intermediate state between death and resurrection? What's it like to be a riverbed longing for a river?

The answer is, of course, speculative. The Undiscovered Country is just that — undiscovered. We simply cannot know the details of mysteries that we cannot fully comprehend. However, if we take the Bible and think with the Church through time, then we are not wholly in the dark.

---

165. Ibid.96.
166. I Corinthians 15:44.
167. II Corinthians 5:2-3.
168. Cf. I Corinthians 15:35ff.

127

In the New Testament, both Jesus and Paul apparently accepted the belief that after death, but before resurrection, there was a continuation of consciousness. Take the parable of the "Rich Man and Lazarus." While Jesus' parables need not and should not be taken literally, they do give evidence of his beliefs concerning such things. What is significant for this discussion is that in the afterlife, the Rich Man goes to Hades and the beggar Lazarus goes to "Abraham's side." The point is that the dead are somewhere and they are conscious. This seems to be consistent with Jesus' teaching on the Resurrection recorded in Mark 12. Note what Jesus says to the Sadducees who denied the Resurrection:

> ...have you not read in the Book of Moses, in the account of the burning bush, how God said to [Moses], 'I am the God of Abraham, the God of Isaac, and the God of Jacob'? He is not the God of the dead, but of the living.

This also agrees with what Jesus tells the good thief dying near Him on the cross: "Today you will be with me in Paradise." Today, right now, in the mystery of God, those who have died but who belong to God are with God. God is not the God of the dead, but of the living, and all live to Him.[169] St. Paul's writings about the afterlife parallel that of our Lord. For example, writing to the ancient church of Philippi, Paul could say:

> I eagerly expect and hope that I will in no way be ashamed, but will have sufficient courage so that now as always Christ will be exalted in my body, whether by life or by death. For to me, to live is Christ and to die is gain. If I am to go on living in the body, this will mean fruitful labor for me. Yet what shall I choose? I do not know! I am torn between the two: I desire to depart and be with Christ, which is far better....[170]

---

169. Luke 20:37-38.
170. Philippians 1:20ff.

Obviously Paul thought that when he died, he and all others who died in Christ would be "with Christ." The well-known and influential New Testament scholar, N.T. Wright, who has done an exhaustive study of the literature, states bluntly that Paul clearly believed that those who have died in Christ are "happy and content."[171] Present with the Risen Lord Jesus, the blessed dead await the Resurrection in God's promised future.

Other Countries in the Post-Mortem World

But where are those who are not with the Lord? The two other destinations in the post-mortem world which receive the most attention are Hell and Purgatory. Our tour of Hell will be short. C.S. Lewis said it as well as anyone:

> ...there is no doctrine which I would more willingly remove from Christianity than this, if it lay in my power. But [1] it has the full support of Scripture, and [2] especially, of Our Lord's own words; [3] it has always been held by Christendom [thus three arguments from authority]; and [4] it has the support of reason.[172]

How is Hell reasonable? Suffice it to say that Hell is reasonable because evidently some people choose to reject God. As a matter of fact, without God's grace, we all would choose to reject God! Hell is not the place that God sends us. It is the place we fallen, broken, and sinful beings send our selves. To quote C.S. Lewis again: "The doors of Hell are locked on the inside."[173]

---

171. N.T. Wright, *The Resurrection of the Son of God* (Minneapolis: Fortress, 2003) 367.

172. C.S. Lewis, *The Problem of Pain* (New York: Macmillan, 1962), 118.

173. Ibid. 127.

Purgatory

As soon as a coin into the coffer rings.
A soul from Purgatory springs! — Father Tetzel O.P.

(Tetzel used this rhyme to sell indulgences to people in 16th century Germany who wanted to secure favor for their deceased loved ones who were, presumably, suffering in Purgatory.)

What about Purgatory? Traditionally, most Protestants have totally rejected the idea of Purgatory. The 18th century American theologian Jonathan Edwards is a good representative of the traditional Protestant understanding:

At death the believer not only gains a perfect and eternal deliverance from sin and temptation, but is adorned with a perfect and glorious holiness. The work of sanctification is then completed, and the beautiful image of God has then its finishing strokes by the pencil of God, and begins to shine forth with a heavenly beauty like a seraphim.[174]

This means that "...the work that believers in the broader [Roman] Catholic tradition ascribe to purgatory is, for most Protestants, accomplished immediately, and apparently painlessly, by a unilateral act of God at death."[175] While this explanation will satisfy most Protestants, it is interesting to note that other Protestants question this. For example, Jerry Walls writes:

...no one can be exempted from the requirement of achieving perfect sanctity in cooperation with God's grace and initiative ... as beings who exist in time, our transformation must be a cooperative venture. It takes time to gain understanding of the various layers of our sinfulness and self-deception, as well as to own the truth about

---

174. As quoted by Jerry L. Walls in "Purgatory for Everyone," *First Things* 122 (April, 2002), 27.

175. Ibid. 27.

ourselves. Discerning truth and allowing it to transform our character is an essentially mental experience that requires time. The doctrine of purgatory makes clear that there is no shortcut to sanctity.[176]

In other words, Purgatory gives us the time we need to prepare to see God face-to-face.[177] From this perspective, Purgatory provides a grace period in which we learn not to hide from God. C.S. Lewis, a Protestant, put it like this:

> Our souls *demand* Purgatory, don't they? Would it not break the heart if God said to us, "It is true, my son, that your breath smells and your rags drip with mud and slime, but we are charitable here and no one will upbraid you with these things, nor draw away from you. Enter into the Joy"? Should we not reply, "With submission, Sir, and if there is no objection, I'd *rather* be cleansed first." "It may hurt, you know." — "Even so, Sir."[178]

If we believe that Purgatory is part of post-mortem existence, then it must be viewed as a "process" of preparation and not as a time of punishment. The punishment for sin was dealt with on the cross of Christ. Jesus was "wounded for our transgressions, crushed for our iniquities; upon him was the punishment that made us whole."[179]

When we turn to the Bible, one passage that may shed some light on this discussion is found in Paul's first letter to the Church at Corinth. This passage is often interpreted in a way that perhaps lends itself to the notion of Purgatory. Paul writes that each of us is called to work to fulfill the purposes of Christ in this life. In the end, all of our works will be judged (not for salvation, but for rewards). This is how Paul puts it:

---

176. Ibid. 29.

177. On the question of whether there is "time" in Heaven, see Peter Kreeft, *Every Think You Ever Wanted to Know About Heaven*, pages 151-162.

178. C.S. Lewis, *Letters to Malcolm* (New York: Harcourt Brace Jovanovich, 1973), 108-109.

179. Isaiah 53:5.

If any person builds on this foundation [Jesus Christ] using gold, silver, costly stones, wood, hay, or straw, their work will be shown for what it is because the Day of Judgment will bring it to light. It will be revealed with fire, and the fire will test the quality of each person's work. If what they have built survives, they will receive their reward. If it is burned up, they will suffer loss; they themselves will be saved, but only as one escaping through the flames (I Corinthians 3:12-5).

Apparently, Paul is writing about a "judgment of cleansing" (purgation) which is distinct from the "judgment of damnation" (hell).

One thing is absolutely certain: Our salvation does not depend on speculations about Purgatory. In the end, we can only echo the words of St. Paul, "I am convinced that neither death, nor life...will be able to separate us from the love of God in Christ Jesus our Lord."[180] God's love is stronger than death. What lies beyond this world and what God has prepared for those who love Him is a wonderful mystery. What we hold with "certain hope" is that Resurrection is truly our destiny.

---

180. Romans 8:38-39.

Questions for Discussion

1. What losses have you experienced in your life? Can you share about your loss? What, if anything, brings you comfort?

2. What does Jesus' resurrection mean to you? What questions or doubts do you have about the Resurrection?

3. Give a brief overview of the understanding of the "resurrection of the body and the immortality of the soul" presented in this chapter. Does it surprise you to learn that the Christian Church does not believe in the innate immortality of the soul?

4. What did you think of Richard Neuhaus' near death experience (NDE)? Do you think this was a real encounter with angels? What did you find most compelling in his story? Have you, or someone you know, ever had an NDE?

5. If you could ask God one question about Heaven, what would it be?

6. Do you believe in Hell? Why or why not?

7. Do you believe in Purgatory? Why or why not?

Chapter 7

What about Mary and the Saints?
The Communion of Saints

If we are brothers and sisters in Christ, we are also brothers of Christ and, therefore, in some important way, sons and daughters of Mary, the mother of Jesus who is the Christ.
— Richard John Neuhaus

Since we are surrounded by such a great cloud of witnesses ... let us run with perseverance the race marked out for us.
— Hebrews 12:1

Let all the saints terrestrial sing,
With those to glory gone;
For all the servants of our King,
In earth and heaven, are one. — John Wesley

I got a phone call from my Mom. I was surprised because she never called too much. It was great to hear her voice. Then, suddenly, I remembered that she was dead.

It was a dream. I can't even remember what she said. After the first couple of sentences I dropped the phone in a faint. I tried to speak, "Mom, but you're...." I couldn't finish. I woke up. Weird.

These kinds of dreams are relatively common. When we lose someone we love, we desire so much to hear and see them again. Dreams sometimes fulfill that wish. The skeptic will argue that all such things are simply wish fulfillment. They're probably right.

However, if there's any truth with what was said in the last chapter, then we'll at least want to ask some more questions. What if the dead make a post-mortem appearance now and then? Do Christians believe in ghosts?

First, there's a word of caution. Echoing the Bible, the Christian Tradition has always looked unfavorably upon any attempts to contact the dead through mediums, Ouija Boards, séances, and other occult methods. There's something unseemly and tainted with all things like this.

But much more positively, in the creeds (the rule of faith), Christians confess faith in the "communion of saints." We rub shoulders with the saints on earth, and mysteriously also rub souls with the saints in heaven. If the blessed dead are with Christ, and Christ is with us, they can't be too far away.

This belief has led many Christians to ask those saints in heaven to pray for the saints on earth. We ask for their prayer support much like we ask the living to pray for us. Should we do this?

Protestants and Roman Catholics are historically very much divided on this issue. For Roman Catholics invoking the saints is as good and natural as asking a living person to pray for us. Even more so because the blessed saints see things more clearly than we do. For Protestants it smacks of superstition. "Why," Protestants ask, "should we beseech the dead when we have the living God to Whom to turn in prayer?" Also, Protestants ask, "Where is the promise in Scripture that such prayers can be heard by the saints who from their labors rest?"

I've spent a lot of time reading and thinking about such questions. My conclusion is that the place to begin is with Mary, the Mother of our Lord. Christians have been seeking her aid in prayer for a very long time. Perhaps she is the missing link which can unite the divided chain of the Church. All catholic Christians consider her to be the Saint *par excellence*. So, let's begin at the point where most Christians agree. Let's begin with the Bible.

The Biblical Mary

The Madonna is not pleased when she is put above her Son. — Pope John XXIII

[Mary in the Magnificat] does not say, "My soul magnifies itself" or "exalts me." She does not desire herself to be esteemed; she magnifies God alone and gives all glory to Him. — Martin Luther, 1521

Some may be surprised that apart from the narratives of Christ's Nativity, Mary is rarely mentioned in the New Testament. However, when she does make an appearance, we should pay attention. She's important.

The earliest mention of Mary in the Bible is found in Paul's letter to the Galatians, written around 48 A.D.: "When the fullness of time had come, God sent forth his Son, born of a woman, born under the law" (4:4). Jesus really was a human being born at a historically particular time into a specifically Jewish family. The biblical Mary was, to state the obvious, Jesus' Mother.

In the Gospel of John, Mary says some of the most profound and wise words in the entire Bible. At the wedding in Cana, she instructs the servants at the wedding, "Do whatever [Jesus] tells you." This is the only advice Mary ever directly gives. We listen to her best when we do whatever her Son tells us to do. In other words, the biblical Mary always points us to her Son, not to herself. As many Roman Catholic theologians have noted, Mary is not pleased when people put her above her Son.

Mary also, as everyone knows, plays a key role in the Christmas stories. She has been prepared and chosen by God to bear the Messiah.[181] The Nativity stories in Matthew and Luke are particularly rich sources for Marian reflection. The first

---

181. Or in Greek, "Christ."

chapter of Luke's Gospel records the story of the angel Gabriel coming to Mary hailing her as the "favored one."[182] The word translated "favored one" has caused some confusion. The root of the word is *grace*. So, another translation has the angel say, "Hail Mary, full of grace." This means that God has been at work in Mary. She was, as Luther said, "God's workshop." God was mightily and graciously at work within her and apparently had been for a long time. The angel's greeting forms the first part of the traditional "Hail Mary" prayer.

After hearing the angel's message, Mary is puzzled because she is a virgin.[183] However, in the end she puts aside her questions and lack of understanding and simply and faithfully responds: "Here am I, the servant of the Lord; let it be with me according to your word."[184] She believes. She trusts. She gives herself to God.

It is by grace through Mary's faith that God takes flesh and comes into the world. Luke Timothy Johnson highlights the importance of Mary's faithful response by drawing our attention to her "symbolic" function in the Nicene Creed:

> ...Mary and Pontius Pilate represent the human race, and, as with so much in the creed, they do so in mythic and balanced fashion. Pilate stands for the world that rejects the claims of God and kills God's messenger who bodily bears that claim. Mary stands for the world that accepts the claim of God and gives birth to the embodiment of God's presence in Jesus the Messiah.[185]

If Mary stands for those who accept the claim of God and give birth to the embodiment of God's presence in this world, then

---

182. Luke 1:28.

183. Luke 1:34.

184. Luke 1:38.

185. Luke Timothy Johnson, *The Creed* (New York: Doubleday, 2003), 159.

all Christians are called to be "Marian" Christians. We, like Mary, are called to say "Yes" to God in order to be part of what God is doing in the world.

After Mary accepts the angel's promise, Luke tells us that she went to visit her cousin Elizabeth, mother of John the Baptist, who was also pregnant. When Elizabeth hears Mary's greeting, she is filled with the Holy Spirit and says, "Blessed are you among women, and blessed is the fruit of your womb."[186] These words form the middle part of the Hail Mary prayer. According to Elizabeth, Mary will hold a place of preeminence for she is "blessed among women."

Later, the familiar words "Pray for us sinners now and at the hour of our death" were added. It's the addition of that last phrase that causes ecumenical problems — problems to which we will turn shortly.

Sometimes the Bible portrays Mary as misunderstanding what her son is doing.[187] Like any mother she is greatly concerned for her son. Most of us can find some comfort in her confusion. She was truly a human being like the rest of us. Any of us who have children know what it's like to sometimes be confused and concerned by their behavior. Mary is the mother of Jesus.

There is a passage in the Revelation of John, chapter 12, which speaks of Mary:

A great portent appeared in heaven: a woman clothed with the sun, with the moon under her feet, and on her head a crown of twelve stars. She was pregnant and was crying out in birth pangs, in the agony of giving birth. Then another portent appeared in heaven: a great red dragon, with seven heads and ten horns, and seven diadems on his heads. His tail swept down a third of the

---

186. Luke 1:43.
187. Mark 3:31-35 and parallels.

stars of heaven and threw them to the earth. Then the dragon stood before the woman who was about to bear a child, so that he might devour her child as soon as it was born. And she gave birth to a son, a male child, who is to rule all the nations with a rod of iron. But her child was snatched away and taken to God and to his throne; and the woman fled into the wilderness, where she has a place prepared by God.

While the "the woman" spoken of here is probably an image of both Mary and the Church, there is a undoubtedly a Marian theme in the mind of the author. While the symbolism contained in the Revelation is often befuddling and difficult, taking this passage at face value we learn that the woman (Mary) fled into wilderness where she has "a place prepared by God."[188] Mary is, therefore, specially protected by God — and mysteriously exalted.

Finally, Mary is mentioned in the Acts of the Apostles. She is with the early Church in prayer.[189]

With this all-too-brief survey of some of the most important "Marian" passages in the New Testament, let's look at what Martin Luther and the Lutheran Confessions say about Mary and the saints. It's important to know that what Luther and the Lutheran Confessions say about Mary and the saints is representative of what most Protestants believe.

Luther and the Lutheran Confessions on Mary and the Saints

Martin Luther's devotion to Mary is well known, and the Lutheran confessional writings continue to honor her as the *theotokos*, the "Mother of God" (*Formula of Concord*, VII, 12). She is also named "ever virgin" (*Smalcald Articles*, I:4). In heaven she, and all the blessed saints, pray for the Church

---

188. Revelation 12:6.
189. Acts 1:14.

on earth (*Apology of the Augsburg Confession*, XXI, 27). Luther would certainly have concurred with the insight of Richard John Neuhaus: "If we are brothers and sisters in Christ, we are also brothers and sisters of Christ and, therefore, in some important way, sons and daughters of Mary, the mother of Jesus who is the Christ."[190]

Now, here's the question: "Should we ask our Mother (or other saints) to speak to her Son on our behalf?" The Lutheran Confessions warn against the practice. *The Augsburg Confession* says that, "it cannot be demonstrated from Scripture that a person should call upon the saints or seek help from them."[191] The Lutheran Confessions limit our devotion to Mary and the Saints to three things:

1. The first is thanksgiving: we ought to give thanks to God because he has given examples of his mercy, because he has shown that he wants to save humankind, and because he has given teachers and other gifts to the church. Since these are the greatest gifts, they ought to be extolled very highly, and we ought to praise the saints themselves for faithfully using these gifts just as Christ praises faithful managers (Matt. 25: 21, 23).

2. The second kind of veneration is the strengthening of our faith. When we see Peter forgiven after his denial, we, too, are encouraged to believe that grace truly superabounds much more over sin (Rom. 5:20).

3. The third honor is imitation: first of their faith, then of their other virtues, which people should imitate according to their callings.[192]

The invocation of Mary and the saints is noticeably absent from this short list. The 16th century Protestant Reformers were

---

190. Richard John Neuhaus, in *Mary: A Catholic-Evangelical Debate*, by Dwight Longenecker and David Gustafson (Grand Rapids: Brazos Press, 2003), 11.

191. Article XXI, 58. Also see I Timothy 2:5.

192. Ibid. *Apology of the Augsburg Confession*, XXI, 237ff.

highly suspicious of the widespread practice of invoking the saints. What gave rise to this suspicion and ultimate rejection?

Should Protestants Pray the Hail Mary?

Five hundred years ago, the devotion to and veneration of the saints was providing the Church with a lucrative source of revenue through the buying, selling, displaying, and veneration of relics. These relics consisted of physical artifacts — perhaps a tooth or piece of bone — that supposedly belonged to deceased saints. The veracity of these relics was often dubious if not outright fraudulent. A relic was thought to possess a semi-magical quality that provided direct access to the departed saint and the help the saint could provide through intercessions. These intercessions were important because in the minds of many, Christ was seen as a distant and rather dangerous Deity who was best approached indirectly. So the faithful sought the influence of the intercessions of his Mother and the other saints. Certainly, thought the Protestant Reformers, this theological canard of an angry Son and a gentle Mother is wholly unbiblical and must be rejected. (Think of it like asking Mom to ask Dad if you can have the car because if you go directly to Dad yourself he'll probably say no.)

Another cause of grave concern for the Protestant Reformers was that the line between *venerating* the saints and *worshiping* the saints was sometimes crossed. The official teaching of the Roman Catholic Church was, and still is, that Mary should be highly venerated (*hyperdulia*) and other canonized saints should be venerated (*dulia*), but neither Mary nor any other saint should be worshiped (*latria*). Only the triune God is worshiped. However, these fine theological distinctions were not always understood or heeded by the faithful. It sometimes looked like idolatry.

Yet another practice that concerned Protestants was the belief that the saints were so holy that they actually had excess holiness to give to the less sanctified. Christians could tap into this treasury of merit and move up on the ladder toward heaven.

142

In other words, the saints were often seen not just as "mediators of intercession, but "mediators of propitiation and redemption."[193] This is a key point.

It was not just a question of whether we were in communion with the saints and could invoke their prayers much like we ask other living saints on Earth to pray for us. The Big Question was whether the saints actually merited or earned salvation for themselves and for others.

The idea that the saints could merit salvation along with Christ was intolerable to the Protestant Reformers because it was in clear violation of a central tenet of the New Testament: "There is one God; there is also one mediator between God and humankind, Christ Jesus, himself human, who gave himself a ransom for all."[194] Instead of Mary and the saints pointing us to the "one mediator," she and other Saints were often understood also to be mini-mediators of salvation.

All of this also caused the Protestants to reject the doctrine of Purgatory. Purgatory was presented as a hellish place where Christians burned off the remaining sin which had been forgiven, but from which they were not totally free. This burning off (purgation) process was often depicted in gruesome scenarios. And once again, the Church authorities raised money by selling indulgences and masses to people who wanted to help their deceased relatives in the post-mortem world and relieve their purgatorial pains. Depending on the price, you could buy thousands of years off a loved one's time in Purgatory.[195]

---

193. Gerhard Forde, "Is Invocation of Saints an Adiaphoron?" *The One Mediator, the Saints, and Mary: Lutherans and Catholics in Dialogue VIII*, eds. H. George Anderson, J. Francis Stafford, and Joseph A. Burgess (Minneapolis: Augsburg Fortress, 1992), 332.

194. I Timothy 2:5.

195. Phillip Cary notes that in 1519, more than 9,000 masses were bought in Wittenberg, Germany alone. The mass had become not only a means to secure the well-being of the deceased, but also a commodity which was bought and sold. Cf. Phillip Cary, *Luther: Gospel, Law, and Reformation* (Chantilly, VA: The Teaching Company, 2004), Part I, Lecture 7.

At this point most Protestants (rather smugly) say, "Debate closed. We're right." However, this attitude forgets a central point, "Abuse does not abrogate proper use."[196] This means that just because people invoked the saints *wrongly* does not mean that there is no way to invoke them *rightly.*

Many Roman Catholics also knew that there were abuses which needed correction. Yet they believed we shouldn't throw the baby out with the proverbial bathwater. All of the practices which the Reformers rejected had at least some biblical warrant, and were supported by the Church's Tradition. Even the power of saintly relics found support in the book of Acts in which we read that God worked miracles through Paul and "even handkerchiefs or aprons that touched his skin were carried away to the sick, and their diseases left them and evil spirits came out of them."[197] It is easy to see how stories like these would lead to the idea that physical objects belonging to a deceased saint would have some kind of power. Of course, it's also easy to see how such ideas would foster superstition and fakery.

The invocation of the saints was an ancient and venerable practice. It had biblical support in the book of II Maccabees[198] and also in the Revelation of St. John. In the Revelation the martyred saints are depicted as under an altar in heaven where they cry out, "Sovereign Lord, holy and true, how long will it be before you judge and avenge our blood on the inhabitants of the earth."[199] Certainly they cry out for all their brothers and sisters who suffer for their faith. Why not ask them to cry out to God for us?

---

196. Ibid. Forde, 335.

197. Acts 19:11-12.

198. A work accepted into the canon by Roman Catholic and Orthodox Christians, but denied canonical status by Protestants who followed the Jewish canon. Cf. II Macc. 15:14.

199. Revelation 6:10.

A Third Way?

So then, is there any wiggle room between these two views? Or, are the classical Protestant and Roman Catholic views of our relationship with the blessed saints wholly contradictory, mutually exclusive, and irreconcilable? Below are four suggestions for further reflection and discussion:

1. The Mystery of Praying "with" the Saints

It should not be doubted that the Church on Earth is *somehow* united with the Church in Heaven. But how exactly the Church *militant* is in communion with the blessed saints in the Church *triumphant* is a mystery. Suppose we ask a particular saint to pray for us. How do they "hear the prayers of individuals" or "discern the silent thoughts of our minds"?[200] We certainly do not want to ascribe omniscience or omnipresence to the blessed dead! Still, at the same time, by faith we affirm that there is a real communion between the saints in Heaven and on Earth. To quote another popular hymn:

> Yet she on earth has union
> with God the Three in One
> And mystic sweet communion
> *with* those whose rest is won.[201] (emphasis added)

This "mystic sweet communion" shared by the saints on Earth *with* the saints in Heaven is a mystery of faith, but it is a "sweet" mystery of faith. To paraphrase the Bard, "There are more things in heaven and on earth than are dreamt of in our *theology*."

In public worship Protestant Christians have rightly argued that we should address our prayers to God alone, but we also remember that our prayers are joined *with* "angels and archangels and all the company of heaven." Included in that com-

---

200. *Article* XXI, lines 10-11: The Invocation of the Saints, *Apology of the Augsburg Confession*.

201. *The Lutheran Book of Worship*, "The Churches One Foundation," #369.

pany are undoubtedly Mary, the Mother of our Lord, and the many blessed saints. We pray with them.

Timothy George, an ordained minister of the Southern Baptist Convention and the dean of Beeson Divinity School, offers the following prayer as an example of praying with Mary:

> Heavenly Father, because in choosing the Blessed Virgin Mary to be the mother of your Son, you exalted the little ones and the lowly. Your angel greeted her as highly favored; and with all generations we call her blessed and *with* her we rejoice and we magnify your holy name.[202]

2. Praying "into" the Company of the Saints

We join our prayers *with* all the saints in Heaven and on Earth. We exist *in* the company of a "great cloud of witnesses" who surround us.[203] We believe, as we confess in the creeds, in the "communion of saints." This means that the saints on earth and the saints in heaven are our *companions*. Literally the word companion means "one with whom we share bread." We share the bread of life, the body and blood of Christ our Companion which sustains us here and, in some sense, hereafter.[204]

To join our prayers "into" the communion of saints in heaven means that we immerse ourselves in their supportive presence as fully human beings who lived, suffered, and died like we all do, but who, "fought the good fight, finished the race, and kept the faith."[205] We see things "dimly" through the eyes of faith. They now see things much more clearly.[206] They have walked ahead of us and know the arduous journey of this

---

202. Timothy George, "Evangelicals and the Mother of God," *First Things* 170 (February 2007), 25.

203. Hebrews 12:1.

204. John 6:41ff. and Revelation 5:6ff.

205. II Timothy 4:7.

206. I Corinthians 13:12.

life. We can relate to the sorrows and struggles they experienced on Earth. Let me give you one example.

As far as we know, Jesus never experienced a prolonged, chronic, life-threatening illness. He certainly knew the agonies of suffering and a cruel death, but He did not personally experience some of the insidious diseases which plague humankind. However, many saints *have* experienced the plethora of human ills and by faith shared their suffering in union with Jesus. These saints can be wonderful helpers to those who also experience similar trials. James Martin wisely writes:

> All the saints encountered suffering of some kind, and when we undergo similar difficulties it's consoling to know not only that there were Christians who underwent such trials, but also that, united with God, the saints are able to pray for us as we suffer.
>
> For example, Therese of Lisieux and Bernadette Soubirous struggled with serious illness in their short lives, as did Pedro Arrupe in his long life. In the face of discouragement about sickness, you might take comfort in the admission of Therese that even she got discouraged, or in the stalwart trust of Bernadette, or in Pedro Arrupe's desire to place himself in "the hands of God." In knowing their lives, you can avail yourself of the saints' wisdom. Like an experienced traveler, a saint can guide you along the path of suffering.[207]

Praying "into" the saints is a way of connecting our life experiences with those who have gone before us "along the path of suffering." The support of the saints in prayer as we contemplate their lives and as we get "into" their experiences should

207. James Martin, SJ, *My Life with the Saints* (Chicago: Loyola Press, 2006), 374-375.

not be lightly dismissed. This type of "veneration" is given tacit approval in the Lutheran confessions.[208]

3. Praying "for" the Saints

In a little book entitled *For All the Saints*, the New Testament scholar and Anglican Bishop N.T. Wright considers the thorny question of whether we should pray *for* our loved ones who have died. Here again, for many Christians the answer will be "Of course! I prayed for them when they were alive and will continue to do so." Other Christians will say that our prayers cannot help the deceased for, as the Bible says, "It is appointed for people to die once, after this comes the judgment."[209] Death ends any opportunity to repent.

The concern of the 16th century Protestant Reformers was that many Christian people lived in a perpetual state of anxiety about the souls of their departed loved ones. What if you thought your beloved family member was suffering in Purgatory, and you could assist them with masses and prayers, but did not? Who would not pay for masses to be said "for" the sake of a beloved family member or friend in order to rescue them from the pains of purgation? But once the idea of dreadful pain and punishment is removed from the concept of Purgatory, and replaced with the concept of growth and continuing sanctification; then things become less problematic for Protestants.

Here is where the thinking of Bishop Wright is again very helpful. He reflects on what it means to pray "for" someone:

> True prayer is an overflowing of love; if I love someone,
> I will want to pray for them, not necessarily because they

---

208. *Augsburg Confession*, Article XXI on The Veneration of the Saints: "The second kind of veneration is the strengthening of our faith. When we see Peter forgiven after his denial, we, too, are encouraged to believe that grace truly superabounds much more over sin (Rom.5:20)." When we venerate the saints we see God's grace in them to strengthen their faith during times of trial and temptation. God promises this same assistance to us.

209. Hebrews 9:27.

are in difficulties, nor necessarily because there is a particular need of which I'm aware, but simply because holding them up in God's presence is the most natural and appropriate thing to do, and because I believe that God chooses to work through our prayers for other people's benefit.... Now love doesn't stop at death — or, if it does, it's a pretty poor sort of love! In fact, grief could almost be defined as the form love takes when the object of love has been removed.... But there is no reason at all why love should discontinue the practice of holding the beloved in prayer before God.[210]

The point I want to emphasize is that when we pray "for" someone it is an expression of love for a person — living or dead — before the throne of God. Certainly when a loved one dies, we do not cease to love them, and their love for us continues. Our prayers for each other are as natural as love itself. What about that loved one who died in apparent sin and unrepentance? Where there is love there is always hope. And even our most firmly held religious dogmas must at least "bend" to love:

> I was a little child when the news came of my father's death, far away. That night, as usual, I prayed for him. But my aunt stopped me. "Darling," she said, "you must not pray for your Father now; it is wrong." And I can remember still how I shrank back, feeling as if someone had slammed the door and shut Father outside.[211]

As we love others, we will pray "for" them. It is not wrong to do so.

---

210. N.T. Wright, *For All the Saints: Remembering the Christian Departed* (Harrisburg, London, New York: Morehouse Publishing, 2003), 73-74.

211. Ingmar Bergman, "The Seventh Seal," in *Four Screenplays by Ingmar Bergman,* as quoted by Peter Kreeft in *Love is Stronger than Death* (San Francisco: Ignatius, 1992), 108.

4. Invocation "of" the Saints

Now we come to the question that tends to divide Christians. Is it permitted for Christians to "invoke" the saints in Heaven and to seek their prayers? Most Protestant Christians will answer, "Why should we since we have Christ Himself as our Mediator and Intercessor?" But for Catholic and Orthodox Christians the answer will certainly be, "Why should we not ask for their prayers just like we ask for each other's prayers?" If "the prayers of a righteous person avails much,"[212] then we must ask whether or not the prayers of the saints in Heaven are "likely to be less effective than the prayers of the saints on Earth?"[213] In seeking to respond to this question, we need to remember the abuses mentioned earlier. The place of devotion to the saints must never replace the devotion due to God alone.

On the positive side, we have established that it is at least permissible to pray "with, into, and for" the faithful who have gone before us. If we take the communion of saints seriously, if we truly believe that our prayers are joined "with" and "into" a great invisible cloud of witnesses who pray "for" one another, then I believe that it is at least *permissible* to ask for the aid of their prayers. Invocation of the saints, asking for their prayers, can even be a sign of a Christian's confidence that Christ has truly defeated death, and therefore the blessed saints enjoy a unique vantage point. They *are* part of our "prayer chain." An obvious danger is that we may spend more time invoking the saints than praying to God! However, concern for *wrongly* invoking the saints should not be the reason given for *never* invoking the saints. Writing of Mary, the Lutheran theologian Robert Jenson says:

> Mary ... has a title, "the Virgin," in order for the church to call on her, to invoke the ministry of one "higher than the cherubim, more glorious than the seraphim." That Prot-

---

212. James 5:16.

213. Geoffrey Wainwright, *Doxology*, 110.

150

estants often avoid wrongly invoking the Virgin by not doing it at all, is a great loss and offends against the creed.[214]

But, if Protestants fail to invoke Mary due to fear of doing so wrongly, then how do we invoke her (or any of the saints) rightly? I think the answer — as in so much else — is love.

What Robert Jenson seems to be saying is that Protestants generally offend against Christian faith when we fail to recognize God's love for Mary, Mary's love for God, and her maternal love for the body of her Son, the Church. Perhaps many of our theological differences about Mary would be greatly resolved if we simply love her and seek to imitate the spiritual beauty of the woman who by God's grace consented through faith to become the Mother of God. When this love is present, then the simple request, "Pray for us," seems to flow quite naturally.

---

214. Robert W. Jenson, *A Large Catechism*, Second Edition (Delhi, NY: American Lutheran Publicity Bureau, 1999), 24.

Questions for Discussion

1. If you grew up in a Christian church, how were Mary and the saints honored?

2. According to John 2, what is the one word of advice that Mary gives?

3. Read Luke 1:26-38. How do you think Mary felt? Do you think she had a choice in the matter? Could she have said no?

4. If you have a devotion to Mary or one of the other great saints, how do you live out that devotion?

5. Does the Marian devotion of other Christians make you "uncomfortable"? Why or why not?

6. According to the Lutheran Confessions, what are the three "primary" reasons to honor the saints?

7. How do you feel about invoking the prayers of the saints in heaven?

8. Do you believe in ghosts?

Chapter 8
What about the Church?

The holiest moment of the church service is the moment when God's people — strengthened by preaching and sacrament — go out of the church door into the world to be the Church. We don't go to church; we are the Church. — Ernest Southcott

One of our great allies at present is the Church itself. Do not misunderstand me. I do not mean the Church as we see her spread out through all time and space and rooted in eternity, terrible as an army with banners. That, I confess, is a spectacle which makes our boldest tempters uneasy. But fortunately it is quite invisible to these humans. — C.S. Lewis, *The Screwtape Letters*

(Screwtape, a senior demon, is instructing a junior demon on how to tempt and trap human prey.)

So we've come to the end of this little journey. Not all questions were answered, and none to everyone's satisfaction. We live by faith, not certainty. Yet, even without absolute certainty (which is unavailable to us in this life) each of us must make decisions. Now the reader must decide: What about the Church?

No Christian can remain isolated from the Church. We're called to be part of a flesh-and-blood community with all the difficulties that brings. The French atheistic philosopher Jean Paul Sartre famously wrote, "Hell is other people." However, it's also true that, "Hell is isolation from other people." When push comes to shove, we need each other. Hence, the Church.

In the first chapter it was noted that most Protestant Christians have always understood themselves to be members of the one, holy, catholic, and apostolic Church. In other words, Protestants have always insisted that they are part of the true Church established by Jesus.[215] We also acknowledged that the one, holy, catholic, and apostolic Church exists outside the confessional boundaries of any particular denomination. In one of the central confessional documents of the Lutheran Church, *The Augsburg Confession*, we read:

> It is taught that at all times there must be and remain one holy, Christian church. It is the assembly of all believers among whom the gospel is purely preached and the holy sacraments administered in conformity with the divine Word. It is not necessary for the true unity of the Christian church that uniform ceremonies, instituted by human beings, be observed everywhere.[216]

In this definition of the Church you will notice several important points:

First, churches do not have to do everything exactly the same way. There is room in *the Church* for differences in *the churches*. It is not necessary that all pastors/priests wear exactly the same robes or that congregations sing the same songs or even believe *exactly* the same things on issues of secondary importance. At the same time, caution is needed.

While it is true that "ceremonies instituted by human beings" may vary and change, it is also necessary to recognize that "worship influences doctrine, and doctrine worship."[217] In other words, what we do and say and sing during worship is

---

215. Matthew 16:13-20.

216. Article VII, Concerning the Church, *The Book of Concord*, Eds. Robert Kolb and Timothy J. Wengert, translated by Charles Arand, Eric Gritsch, Robert Kolb, William Russell, James Schaaf, Jane Strohl, Timothy J. Wengert (Minneapolis: Fortress Press, 2000), 42.

217. Geoffrey Wainwright, *Doxology: The Praise of God in Worship, Doctrine and Life* (New York: Oxford, 1980), 218.

a confession of what we believe *and how we live*. Worship forms and shapes our faith and life in subtle, but important ways. Changes to the Church's historic liturgy must never be done haphazardly. To abandon altogether the historic liturgy of the Church is a move in the direction of sectarianism. Our faith and life are influenced by the ways we worship. Consider the following:

> People attend worship with expectations shaped by television, and evangelical preachers try to meet them. In such cases worship may degenerate into a religious variety show hosted by some gleaming evangelist in a sequined dinner jacket and patent leather dancing slippers who chats with celebrities and introduces for special music a trio of middle-aged women in pastel evening gowns with matching muffs for their microphones. He may also include, or even perform, certain eye-popping acrobatics or karate moves. Each act in the show is pre-timed, including estimates of the length of audience applause. Imagine a High Five for Jesus replacing the Apostles' Creed.[218]

What kind of Christian faith and life is nurtured and developed when worship becomes a "religious variety show"? Or when a "High Five for Jesus" replaces the Apostles' Creed? Certainly not the Christian faith. Again, 'ceremonies instituted by humans beings" may vary from place to place and time to time. However, worship centering on the stage and the audience and entertainment is *not* Christian worship. When the "audience" replaces the congregation and the "stage" replaces the altar, then there are real theological problems afoot. God has, unfortunately, lost center stage. In truly Christian worship, God is always both the subject and the object of worship. In other words, it's not about you or me. Worship is about God.[219]

---

218. Cornelius Plantinga, Jr., *Not the Way It's Supposed to Be: A Breviary of Sin* (Grand Rapids: William B. Eerdmans, 1995), 192-193.

219. Thanks to the theologian Marva Dawn for noting this essential truth about Christian worship.

Neither is faithful worship the doing of dry and dusty liturgies with little passion and less joy. Let's celebrate the liturgy with reverence and joy by worshiping God in the "beauty of holiness."

Second, the definition of the Church in *The Augsburg Confession* reminds us that the Church of Jesus Christ will endure forever. One of the miracles of God is that after 2,000 years, the Church still exists and often thrives in spite of schisms and heresies and persecutions and various corruptions and stupidities. Jesus said, "The gates of hell will not prevail" against the Church.[220] The Church continues to exist, and in many places thrives, because God is faithful.

Finally, you will find the true Church of Jesus Christ where the Word of God is rightly preached, and the sacraments administered "in conformity with the divine Word." Earlier we thought about the authority of God's written Word, but what about the sacraments? What is a sacrament and how is it to be administered?

The Sacramental Life

It is no doubt something of an offense that I, great spiritual being that I am, should have to depend on being washed or eating a bit of bread and drinking a sip of wine for salvation. But so it is and so it must be preached.
— Gerhard Forde

In one way, every physical thing which communicates God to us is a sacrament. The beauty and grandeur of creation communicate something of the beauty and grandeur of the Creator. The loving word or touch of a friend or family member communicates the truth of God's love. Every created good tells us that there is a Goodness in, with, and under it. The poet Gerard Manley Hopkins, who was also a Jesuit priest, captured this truth so beautifully:

---

220. Matthew 16:18.

THE WORLD is charged with the grandeur of God.
It will flame out, like shining from shook foil;
It gathers to a greatness, like the ooze of oil
Crushed. Why do men then now not reck his rod?
Generations have trod, have trod, have trod;
And all is seared with trade; bleared, smeared with toil;
And wears man's smudge and shares man's smell: the soil
Is bare now, nor can foot feel, being shod.

And for all this, nature is never spent;
There lives the dearest freshness deep down things;
And though the last lights off the black West went
Oh, morning, at the brown brink eastward, springs—
Because the Holy Ghost over the bent
World broods with warm breast and with ah! bright wings.[221]

Human sin smudges God's creation, but it cannot eradicate God's goodness within creation. "Nature is never spent ... because the Holy Ghost over the bent world broods." God's sacramental presence reawakens and renews the earth.

Likewise, sacraments are visible, tangible created "things" which communicate the invisible, intangible gracious presence of God which renews faith. St. Augustine called the sacraments "visible words." Christians don't agree on how many "visible words" there are. Still, the vast majority of Christians believe that there are two major sacraments — baptism and Holy Communion. The Holy Spirit broods over the waters of baptism and bends the bread and wine of the Eucharist into the body and blood of Christ. This sacramental grace cannot ever be "spent" because it bears the unbreakable promise of God. Jesus himself said, "This is my body ... This is my blood." This divine word "attached" to the sacramental element — water, bread, wine — *is* God's good Word which cannot be eradicated. In this sacramental Word God speaks to us of forgiveness, life, and salvation in Christ Jesus.

---

221. Gerard Manley Hopkins, "God's Grandeur."

When these rites are done "in conformity with the divine Word" there is a holy communication. When we find ourselves making the sign of the cross in remembrance of our washing (baptism) and holding out our hands to receive "a bit of bread and a sip of wine" together with a bunch of flawed and imperfect people, then we begin to understand what God is saying to us, and *doing* to us, in the sacraments.

Holy Baptism

One of my first real encounters with Christianity occurred when I was about 10 years old and a neighborhood friend invited me to Sunday School. For whatever reason, I said yes. My mom and stepfather probably thought that a little religion would do me good so off I went. Within a couple of years I discovered confirmation classes were part of the package. So, for about eight weeks I went to a few confirmation classes which ultimately led to my baptism. The only thing I remember about those classes is that we talked about Jesus telling His disciples they should forgive not just seven times but seven times seventy.[222] The Holy Spirit must have known that I would have cause to claim those verses.

I can still remember kneeling at the altar of the church when the Pastor (we called him "Reverend") doused me with a little water in the name of the Father, and the Son, and the Holy Spirit. Then? Nothing happened. At least nothing happened that I perceived. There was a splash of water on my head, the pastor mumbled the triune Name, and that was it. No lights, no visions, no epiphanies. As I entered into my adolescent years it was *almost* entirely forgotten. Maybe my baptism didn't take. It certainly didn't improve my behavior.

Here is perhaps the most important point of baptism: it is not *primarily* about the faith or level of understanding or commitment of the person who is baptized. To be sure, an adoles-

---

222. Matthew 18:22.

158

cent or adult who is baptized must give their consent. They must desire to be baptized and instructed in the Christian faith. But our subjective disposition is secondary to the main point: baptism is primarily something that God does. Or perhaps more accurately, something God says. God speaks and His word creates new life. God begins to bend our bound wills back towards Himself. The doctrine of *original sin* reminds us that we are all born with a narcissistic bent. This is one reason why in most churches even infants are baptized.[223]

Left to ourselves, without the grace of God, "human life degenerates into the clamor of competing autobiographies ... the self exists to be explored, indulged, and expressed but not disciplined or restrained."[224] Baptism tells us something we don't want to hear. The *self* in which life is so often centered must be drowned, killed, and crucified with Christ. Then, and only then, do we begin to live life as God intended, a life in which love for God and neighbor are central.

Even in churches that do not baptize infants but wait until a person reaches an age to make a personal decision, the stress should not be on the strength of the person's subjective faith or commitment — which are extremely fickle in humans. Rather, the emphasis of baptism is on what God has done, is doing, and promises to do in the future. My own lackluster commitment at baptism is a case in point. Later, when I came to a more mature commitment of faith, I started listening to my baptism. Rebaptisms should be avoided because it takes the emphasis away from God's objective promise and puts the emphasis upon our subjective (and often shaky) faith.

---

223. Alas, whether or not infants should be baptized or not is another point over which the churches are divided. However, the vast majority of Christian churches do baptize infants when they are presented by Christian parents or a Christian family who will help the child grow into their baptism.

224. Cornelius Plantinga, Jr., *Not the Way It's Supposed to Be: A Breviary of Sin*, 83.

The entire Christian life is sacramentally enacted in baptism. We are united to Christ, buried with Christ, raised with Christ, washed from sin's stain, and adopted as God's children. To live our baptism is our vocation. The promise of God spoken to us and applied to us with water in the name of the triune God is a promise that is valid *even if we never claim it! Even if, God forbid, we reject it*. It is God's promise to be our dear heavenly Father, to wash us of our sin, and to raise us from the dead to be with Christ.

So, if you've not been baptized, now's your chance. If you were baptized, now's your chance to hear it anew.

Holy Communion

> *Out of the darkness of my life, so much frustrated, I put before you the one great thing to love on earth: the Blessed Sacrament.... There you will find romance, glory, honour, fidelity, and the true way of all your loves on earth, and more than that: Death: by the divine paradox, that which ends life, and demands the surrender of all, and yet by the taste (or foretaste) of which alone can what you seek in your earthly relationships (love, faithfulness, joy) be maintained, or take on that complexion of reality, of eternal endurance, which every man's heart desires.* — J.R.R. Tolkien
> (writing to his son Christopher on the importance of "the Blessed Sacrament" of Holy Communion)

Another story... On Christmas Eve, 1973, I attended midnight Mass with some Catholic friends. I was trying to learn more about Christianity and so this seemed like a good place to begin. The church was packed with worshipers and I was forced to sit a few rows away from my friends. When it came time to receive communion I simply followed everyone else. As I stood in line waiting to receive, my Catholic friends kept motioning for me to sit down. I didn't get it, and was annoyed by their protests. I, a wayward cultural Protestant who came from a family with no strict religious convictions, was going to receive communion in the Roman Catholic Church. Perhaps my friends thought that the Almighty would strike me dead on the spot. However, the priest, who certainly did not know me, communed me (and I lived to tell about it).

The sacrament of Holy Communion is also called the Eucharist, the Lord's Supper, the Sacrament of the Altar, and the Mass. It is observed in almost all Christian traditions. Unfortunately, Christians disagree and are divided over many issues surrounding it.

Perhaps the greatest division is over one question: Is Jesus Christ truly present in Holy Communion? Do we receive the true crucified and glorified body and blood of Christ when we eat and drink at the Lord's Table? Is he really present *for* us in, with, and under the bread and wine?

This is not just a metaphysical or mystical question about which we can have a discussion over cocktails. It is a question of where we really find God. Is Christ objectively present *for us* at the Eucharist? That is, present outside of ourselves and our experiences. Or, is Holy Communion a means to stir up our spiritual affections so that Christ is present in our feelings or experiences of faith? Don't misunderstand me, experiences of God can be good and powerful. The problem is that they come and go. We can't (or at least shouldn't) build our faith on spiritual experiences.

The late Roman Catholic writer Flannery O'Connor understood this. In a letter written to a friend, she describes a dinner party she attended that was given by the lapsed Catholic socialite and intellectual Mary McCarthy and her husband Bowden Broadwater:

> ...I hadn't opened my mouth once, there being nothing in such company for me to say.... Having me there was like having a dog present who had been trained to say a few words but overcome with inadequacy had forgotten them. Well, toward morning the conversation turned on the Eucharist, which I, being the Catholic, was obviously supposed to defend. Mrs. Broadwater said when

161

she was a child and received the Host, she thought of it as the Holy Ghost, He being the "most portable" person of the Trinity; now she thought of it as a symbol and implied that it was a pretty good one. I then said, in a very shaky voice, "Well, if it's a symbol, to hell with it." That was all the defense I was capable of.[225]

Flannery O'Connor recognized the fact that if Holy Communion is *only* a symbol then it is something that we can dispense with. Why? Because Jesus isn't really *sacramentally* present. Where is he? He's in our "hearts" or in the "experience of faith." If that's true, then what matters is that Christian worship tries to help people experience the presence of God emotionally.

What replaces the Eucharist? Feelings, ideas, music, videos, programs, speaking in tongues, sweat lodges with pot and peyote; it doesn't really matter. What matters is that we have a felt experience of God. Now, mystical religious experiences can be of great value, and charismatic gifts like speaking in tongues, healings, and other manifestations of the Spirit are often true signs of God's presence. It's always good to *feel* close to God. But again, feelings are a flimsy foundation on which to build our faith.

The evangelical Protestant, Donald Miller, writes about receiving Holy Communion. Note how he differs from Flannery O'Connor's Roman Catholic (and Lutheran) perspective:

...often, as I wait in line, go to the table, take the bread, and dip it into the cup of wine, I forget that the bread and wine I eat and drink are of absolutely no spiritual significance at all, that they have no more power than the breakfast I ate that morning, that what Jesus wanted was for us to eat the bread and drink the wine as a way of *remembering Him...* (emphasis in original).[226]

---

225. As quoted by Paul Elie in *The Life You Save May be Your Own: An American Pilgrimage* (New York: Farrar, Straus and Giroux, 2003), 176.

226. Donald Miller, *Searching for God Knows What* (Nashville: Nelson Books, 2004), 163.

Note well his emphasis. There is no "spiritual significance," and certainly no "sacramental presence" of Christ in the bread and wine of Holy Communion. What matters is our subjective act of remembering Jesus. Apparently the cognitively impaired could gain nothing from the sacrament. God does not "really" come to us, speak to us, through these tangible elements of bread and wine. God speaks to us in our hearts and minds. One can also imagine O'Connor's response, "Well, if that's all it is, to hell with it."

If Donald Miller is right, then when we gather to remember Jesus it makes little difference "how" or even "if" we receive the bread/body and wine/blood of Holy Communion because again, Jesus isn't there. He's in my subjective thoughts, feelings, and ideas as I remember (think about) him. The Eucharist then becomes a human work rather than a divine gift because it depends upon *my* thoughts and feelings for validity.

Now, I hope it's obvious that remembering and meditating on Christ's death are good things to do. And subjective religious feelings and experiences can be life changing. The problem arises when we begin to think that our meditating and remembering somehow makes the absent Jesus *really* present. We look inside ourselves to find our feelings for Jesus, and soon misplace him. Just try it. Look inside yourself for Jesus. Where did I put him? He was here a moment ago when I *felt* his presence. But what if I don't feel it?

"In Remembrance of Me"

Jesus said, "Do this in remembrance of me." These words are engraved over countless altars and communion tables in countless churches. What did he mean? When a modern person hears the word "remember," she may, like Donald Miller, think to herself: "The bread and wine are of no significance. What matters is that they help me to *remember* that Jesus died for me and I experience his presence." This is perhaps the most commonly held belief among Protestant Christians.

163

However, if this is all that it is, then it is very difficult to avoid Flannery O'Connor's stinging critique. Why bother with bread and wine at all? Why not show a video of *The Passion of the Christ* complete with Hollywood special effects? The movie will certainly help us to remember what Christ suffered and endured for us.

What we must *remember* is that the word *remembrance* used in the Bible does not only mean to be *reminded* of an event or a person. Holy Communion means much more than tying a sacramental string of bread and wine around our finger to remind us that Christ died for us. To remember in the biblical sense means to share in the reality of the event, or person, remembered. In the Bible, the opposite of *remember* is not simply to forget, but to *dismember*.

When a person forgets his or her God, or even worse when a person is forgotten by God, it means that person is dismembered from God's people.[227] To remember Jesus in the sacrament is to be "re-membered" with him and with the community that bears his name. This is why Paul can write in I Corinthians 10:16-17:

> The cup of blessing that we bless, is it not a sharing in the blood of Christ? The bread that we break, is it not a sharing in the body of Christ? Because there is one bread, we who are many are one body for we all partake of the one bread.

Through the Eucharistic bread and wine, we share in Christ's body and blood and are re-membered with Christ and with the people of Christ — the Church. Baptism unites us with Christ, Holy Communion is the sacrament which strengthens our union with Christ. In both, Christ is *really present* to save us.

---

227. Cf. Psalms 25:6-7; 74:2; 106:4; etc.

Should I Receive Holy Communion?

So, if this is "what" the sacrament of Holy Communion is, how do we know *if* we should receive it? The Apostle Paul gave a sharp warning to some who receive communion "in an unworthy manner" and thus sin "against the body and blood of the Lord."[228] So, who is worthy to receive?

I'm reminded of a story told by Father Ronald Rolheiser, a Roman Catholic priest. He writes about a "fallen" Catholic. This lapsed Catholic was a man who had rejected the faith of his family and was living in open and even defiant disregard for the teachings of the Church. Through a series of events including a painful reconciliation with his father, he decided to go back to church. So, he went to see a priest and asked him whether he could simply start coming again and receive communion. The priest told him that he must first go to confession and get his life squared away with God and the Roman Catholic Church before coming to communion. This frustrated and angered the young man, and he left and began to attend a Protestant church. However, he did not find what he needed most in the various congregations he attended. Finally, one Sunday, despite the rules, he just got up and went to Mass and received Holy Communion. For this man, the moment of receiving communion in the Church of his childhood, was a real homecoming. He *felt* forgiven. Father Rolheiser tells this story and then adds his own words of commentary that are insightful for all Christians:

> What this story highlights is something the church has always taught, even in its official teachings, and ... we invariably lose, namely *the eucharist is the primary sacrament of reconciliation* and that *going to eucharist is not a moral statement.* We go to eucharist because we *need* health, not because we *are* healthy.[229]

---

228. I Corinthians 11:27.

229. Ronald Rolheiser, *Against an Infinite Horizon: The Finger of God in Our Everyday Lives* (New York: Crossroads, 2001), 85.

A truer word about who should receive Holy Communion was never spoken. Coming to Holy Communion (the Eucharist) is not a declaration that I have lived such a great life this past week and am worthy to receive the gift of God. No. The truth is that all of us come to Holy Communion filled with a week's worth (or a lifetime's worth) of sin, brokenness, confusion, doubt, fear, and failure. And each time we come, the same promise is spoken: "This is my body given for you. This is my blood shed for you." When we trust those words of promise, we have precisely what they say. We have God "for us."

The answers to life's biggest questions begin and end with grace. This is what makes Christianity truly unique.

Conclusion

In the Introduction I directed this book to people who may consider themselves "spiritual, but not religious." There's a dark side to religion. We see or hear about it on a daily basis. Yet, there's also a light side. The question each of us must ask is whether or not any religious truth is "enlightening" to the human experience. It would be both foolish and dark *not* to follow the light.

As I said earlier, the danger in being spiritual without being religious is that we may enjoy our questions so much that we never really think to find answers. We remain forever curious, but never committed. It's like a hungry person who enjoys looking for food, thinking about food, imagining food; but never actually finding and eating it. At some point the spiritual person must sit down to eat. True religion offers real food for spiritually hungry people. *If* the answers to life's questions proposed by the Christian faith have truth in them, *then* we must make a commitment to be nourished by them.

So, if there's any light, even a small glimmer, in the previous pages, I hope that each of us will take a step in that direction. Ultimately, the light will lead us to the truth — God's Truth.

Endnote on the Church's Ecumenical Witness on the Eucharist

For those who are interested in what the various traditions within the Church catholic teach regarding the sacrament of holy communion, here are some statements by the respective churches:

St. Augustine (Church Father, who represents some of the best thinking of both Protestant and Catholic Christians, d.430): "What you can see here, dearly beloved, on the table of the Lord, is bread and wine; but this bread and wine, when the word is applied to it, becomes the body and blood of the Word."[230]

The Augsburg Confession (Lutheran, 1530): "Concerning the Lord's Supper it is taught that the true body and blood of Christ are truly present under the form of bread and wine in the Lord's Supper and are distributed and received there."[231]

The French Confession of the Reformed Church (1559) which is representative of the "mature" thinking of John Calvin: "We believe that God truly and effectively gives us what is represented in the Lord's Supper ... and that the signs are united with the true possession and benefit of all they present. Thus, all who bring the receptacle of pure faith to the sacred table of Christ truly receive what the signs signify. The body and blood of Jesus Christ are food and drink for the soul just as bread and wine are nourishment for the body."[232]

The United Methodist Church (2004): "Through Jesus Christ and in the power of the Holy Spirit, God meets us at the Table. God, who has given the sacraments to the church, acts in and through Holy Communion. Christ

---

230. *Ancient Christian Commentary on Scripture: New Testament IVa, John 1-10*, edited by Joel C. Elosky, General Editor, Thomas C. Oden (Downers Grove, IL: InterVarsity Press, 2006), 44.

231. Ibid., 44.

232. *The French Confession, 1559*, Article XXXVII.

is present through the community gathered in Jesus' name (Matthew 18:20), through the Word proclaimed and enacted, and through the elements of bread and wine shared (I Corinthians 11:23-26). The divine presence is a living reality and can be experienced by participants; it is not a remembrance of the Last Supper and Crucifixion only."[233]

The Orthodox Churches: "The Eucharist ... is the Mystery [sacrament] in which the bread and wine of offering are changed by the Holy Spirit into the true Body and Blood of our Lord Jesus Christ, and then the believers receive communion of them for a most intimate union with Christ and eternal life."[234]

The Roman Catholic Church: "In the most blessed sacrament of the Eucharist 'the body and blood, together with the soul and divinity, of our Lord Jesus Christ and, therefore, *the whole Christ is truly, really, and substantially contained.*'"[235]

So then, if we look at the ecumenical witness of the churches — even if there are different understandings of *how* Christ is present[236] — there is a clear consensus that the sacrament of Holy Communion is much more than just a simple service of symbolically remembering that Jesus died for us.

---

233. *This Holy Mystery: A United Methodist Understanding of Holy Communion*, adopted by the General Conference of the United Methodist Church, 2004, 16.

234. Protopresbyter Michael Pomazansky, *Orthodox Dogmatic Theology*, trans. by Hieromonk Seraphim Rose, 3rd edition (St. Herman of Alaska Brotherhood, 2005), 279-280.

235. *The Catechism of the Catholic Church*, Part Two, Section 1374, 383.

236. The Lutheran Reformers attempted to explain the "how" of Christ's Real Presence in Holy Communion by teaching the doctrine of the ubiquity of Christ. In other words, after the resurrection the humanity of Jesus (his body and blood) shares in the divine and omnipresent nature of God. The Roman Catholic Church teaches the doctrine of *transubstantiation*. This teaching says that when the bread and wine are consecrated by the priest the *substance* the bread and wine are changed or

Questions for Discussion

1. What have you learned from this study? What is one major question or struggle you have concerning the Christian faith?

2. Where you baptized? If so, where and when?

3. Do you remember anything about your baptism? Do you ever think about it? How could you remember it daily?

4. When and where did you receive your first Holy Communion? Was it important to you at the time?

5. What did Jesus mean when he said, "Do this in remembrance of me?"

6. Do you ever feel unworthy to receive communion? When is a person prepared to receive the sacrament?

7. What does it mean to you to be a Christian? Can you be a Christian without being a member of the Body of Christ, the Church?

8. Have you ever had a bad experience in the Church? Or with a member of the clergy? Do you want to share about it?

9. Are you prepared to become a member of this Christian church? Why or why not?

---

transubstantiated into the body and blood of Christ. However the *accidents* of the bread and wine remained unchanged. This understanding of holy communion draws upon the teaching of the ancient Greek philosopher Aristotle. Aristotle taught that proper distinctions must be made between an object's *substance* and its *essence*. The Theologian Robert Jenson (himself a Lutheran) explains: "Were I at this moment of writing to cease to be mammalian, the writing of this essay would cease because *I* would have ceased; were my hair instantly to turn white, I could carry on writing as the same one I was before. Thus some predicates of any real thing can be seen as belonging to its 'substance,' in the sense that without them the thing would not be at all, while others, 'accidents,' can come and go less portentously." *On Thinking the Human* (Grand Rapids: Eerdmans, 2003), 61. Both Roman Catholics and Lutherans teach the doctrine that Christ, in his body and blood, his humanity and deity, is truly present and received in holy communion.

About the Author

Eric M. Riesen has served as the Senior Pastor of Zion Lutheran Church in Pittsburgh for 21 years, and is Dean Emeritus of the Mid-Northeast Mission District (North American Lutheran Church).

He is a member of the NALC's Joint Commission on Theology and Doctrine and the Lutheran/Anglican Consultation Committee (North American Lutheran Church and the Anglican Church in North America). He holds degrees from Indiana University (B.S.), Fuller Theological Seminary (M.A.), Luther Northwestern Theological Seminary (M.Div.), and Pittsburgh Theological Seminary (D. Min.).

Pastor Riesen is married to Terry Lynne Riesen and they have three grown children.

Made in the USA
Middletown, DE
25 February 2016